WILD ANIMALS WORKBOOK

by Robin Lee Makowski

Illustrated by
Robin Lee Makowski
and
Jael

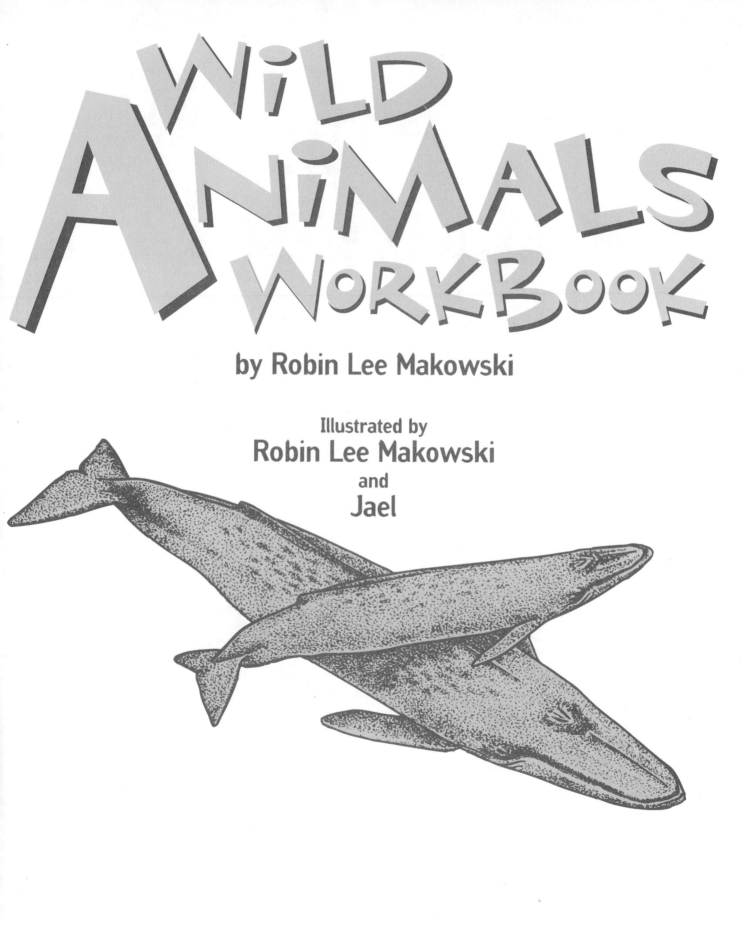

CONTENTS

INTRODUCTION

Do you love animals? You are about to meet hundreds of fascinating creatures: big cats and small spiders, desert bats and South Pole penguins, active eels and extinct dinosaurs.

Each page of this book features a terrific animal-related activity. You'll learn amazing facts as you test your skills in word finds, mazes, and puzzles. You will learn how clownfish escape from predators, where caimans live, and how bats "see" in dark caves. You also will encounter deadly hunters, horned beetles, smiling crocodiles, and many other wild animals.

Are you ready to learn about these spectacular creatures? Then get started on the Wild Animals Workbook right away!

Mysteries of the Deep!

The sea is home to hundreds of thousands of different animals, and that is not counting the creatures that have not yet been discovered! Mammals, birds, reptiles, fish, and other plants and animals thrive in the ocean, which is chock-full of nutrients.

One of the most important nutrients is plankton, which is made up of microscopic plants and animals. Lots of ocean dwellers eat plankton, which puts it at the bottom of the food chain. At the top of the food chain are large, powerful animals that have very few enemies. Some sharks and whales, such as whale sharks and blue whales, eat lots of plankton. Others, such as great white sharks and sperm whales, hunt other animals for food.

Marine animals have adapted to their watery world in many ways. Whales and dolphins, which are mammals, breathe air through a blowhole at the top of their heads. They have a layer of fat under their skin called blubber. This fat keeps them warm in the cold water.

Fish do not breathe air. They use their gills to take oxygen directly from the water. Sharks have rows of sharp teeth that grow back when they break off. Sharks can also push their jaws out of their mouths to get a firm bite on prey. Penguins cannot fly, but they can dive hundreds of feet deep in the water and swim using their feathered wings as flippers. They can stay underwater for up to 18 minutes hunting fish, plankton, and squid.

Answer the questions below by taking hints from the sea-creature facts above. Then unscramble the circled letters to answer the bonus question.

1. Marine _ _ _O_ _ _ have _ _ _O_ _ _ to their watery world.
2. Many sea creatures feed on _ _ _ _ _ _O_.
3. Whales and sharks are at the top of the ocean _O_ _ O_ _O_.
4. Sharks can push their _ _ _O out of their mouths to catch prey.
5. Fish take _ _ _ _ _ _ from the water through their _O_ _ _.
6. Penguins have _ _ _ _ _ _, but they can't fly.
7. _ _ _ _ _ _ _O, a layer of fat, keeps whales warm in the O_ _ _ water.
8. Mammals, fish, birds, and reptiles all thrive in the _O_ _ _ _.

Bonus Question: Some of the largest animals in the world feed on
_ _ _ _ _ _ _ _ _ _ _ plants and animals called plankton.

Too Close to Home!

Your own backyard is a wildlife paradise! From raccoons and rabbits to mosquitoes and moose, wildlife is all around you. People living near forests may have deer and bears in their yards, while city dwellers have pigeons, mice, squirrels, and other small wildlife.

Lots of animal pests also live near people. Flies and roaches often find their way into our homes. Other creatures, such as spiders, snakes, and bats, are helpful backyard neighbors. They feed on rats, flies, and biting mosquitoes.

Depending on where you live, some of the animals below may be found in your backyard. Some are very good at hiding. See if you can find at least 25.

Getting to Know Bats

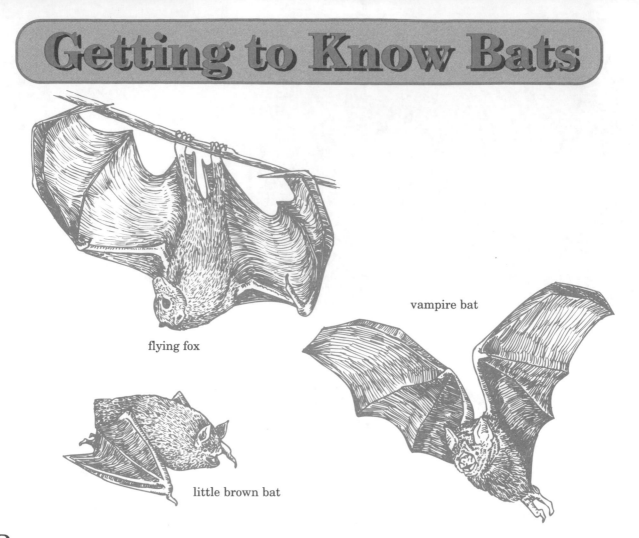

flying fox

vampire bat

little brown bat

Bats are unusual and fascinating animals, long misunderstood by people. There are almost 1,000 different species, or kinds, of bats. They range in size from Thailand's bumblebee bat—the smallest of all flying mammals, which measures two and a half inches long, and fits neatly into a walnut shell—to the flying fox, which has a wingspan of more than six feet.

In ancient times, people thought that bats were featherless birds. But we now know that bats are mammals. They are warm-blooded, they nurse their babies, and have hair or fur. Bats are the only mammals that can fly! Their wings consist of thin sheets of skin stretched among five long finger bones and connected to the hind legs.

Many people believe that bats are blind. Actually, bats can see quite well in the daytime. However, most bats hunt at night, so this is not very helpful. To see in the dark, bats use echolocation *(eh-koh-loh-KAY-shun)*. They send sounds through their noses or mouths that bounce off objects. Bats can hear the echo of the sounds, and this tells them where to find small animals, such as insects, frogs, and fish.

Some people believe that bats are dangerous, but bats do not attack people. Even the blood-thirsty vampire bat, which feeds on the blood of other animals, will not attack a human being. Bats are actually helpful to people and the environment. By distributing pollen and seeds when they feed on flowers and fruits, bats help plants to grow. Also, bats keep certain insects, such as mosquitoes, under control. The little brown bat may catch as many as 1,200 flying insects in one night! If it weren't for bats, the world would be a peskier place.

Your Basic Bat Facts

See what you have learned so far about bats by completing the puzzle below. Fill in the blanks with the correct word. Then make the words fit into the empty boxes beneath. Be careful. Some words may fit into more than one place, but there is only one correct place for them to go.

Bats are the only _ _ _ _ _ _ _ that can fly.
The _ _ _ _ _ _ _ _ _ flying mammal in the world is the _ _ _ _ _ _ _ _ _ _ bat of Thailand.

_ _ _ _ _ _ _ _ _ _ _ _ have wingspans over six feet long.
Bats use _ _ _ _ _ _ _ _ _ _ _ _ _ _ _ to hunt at night.
Bats help plants grow when they feed on _ _ _ _ _ and flowers.
Bats help keep _ _ _ _ _ _ _ _ under control.
The little _ _ _ _ _ _ bat is an insect-eater.
The _ _ _ _ _ _ _ _ bat eats the _ _ _ _ _ of other animals, but is not dangerous to people.

brown bat

bumblebee bat

Did you know that there are more than 6,500 species of reptiles? Some are small enough to fit in your hand, and some are big enough to eat you alive!

Reptiles are cold-blooded animals, which means that they depend on their environment to regulate their body temperature. That is why reptiles can be found on all continents except icy Antarctica. Covered with a scaly layer of armor, these animals are often seen basking in the sun to warm up or hiding in the shade to cool down.

Take a look below and get to know the reptile groups.

MEET THE REPTILES!

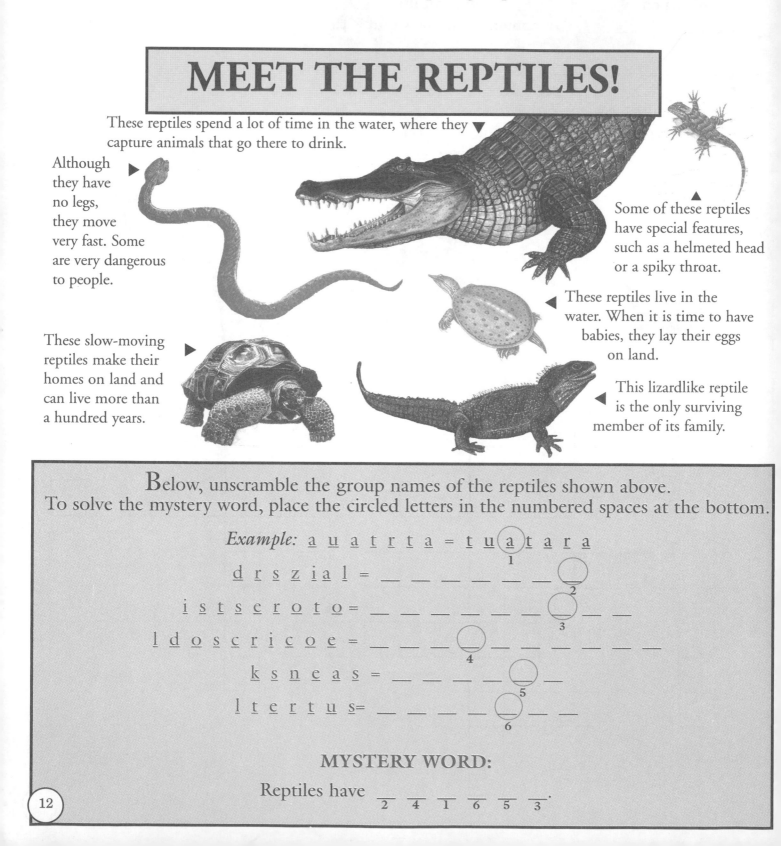

These reptiles spend a lot of time in the water, where they capture animals that go there to drink. ▼

Although they have no legs, they move very fast. Some are very dangerous to people. ▶

Some of these reptiles have special features, such as a helmeted head or a spiky throat. ▲

These reptiles live in the water. When it is time to have babies, they lay their eggs on land. ◀

These slow-moving reptiles make their homes on land and can live more than a hundred years. ▶

This lizardlike reptile is the only surviving member of its family. ◀

Below, unscramble the group names of the reptiles shown above. To solve the mystery word, place the circled letters in the numbered spaces at the bottom.

Example: a u a t r t a = t u a t a r a
                                   (a)
                                    1

d r s z i a l = _ _ _ _ _ _ ◯
                              2

i s t s e r o t o = _ _ _ _ _ _ ◯ _ _
                                  3

l d o s c r i c o e = _ _ _ ◯ _ _ _ _ _ _
                            4

k s n e a s = _ _ _ ◯ _
                      5

l t e r t u s = _ _ _ ◯ _ _
                        6

MYSTERY WORD:

Reptiles have _ _ _ _ _ _.
               2 4 1 6 5 3

The tuatara *(too-uh-TAR-uh)* is called a living fossil because it has stayed pretty much the same since prehistoric times. Also, this lizardlike reptile is the last of its kind, having no other family members still in existence.

The tuatara itself is moving toward extinction. Having no natural enemies, it used to be plentiful throughout New Zealand. But several decades ago, rats were introduced to the tuatara's habitat. Not only do the rats prey on tuatara eggs and babies, but they also compete with adult tuataras for food.

Tuataras will eat almost anything, but one of their favorite foods is the weta, a common ground cricket common in New Zealand.

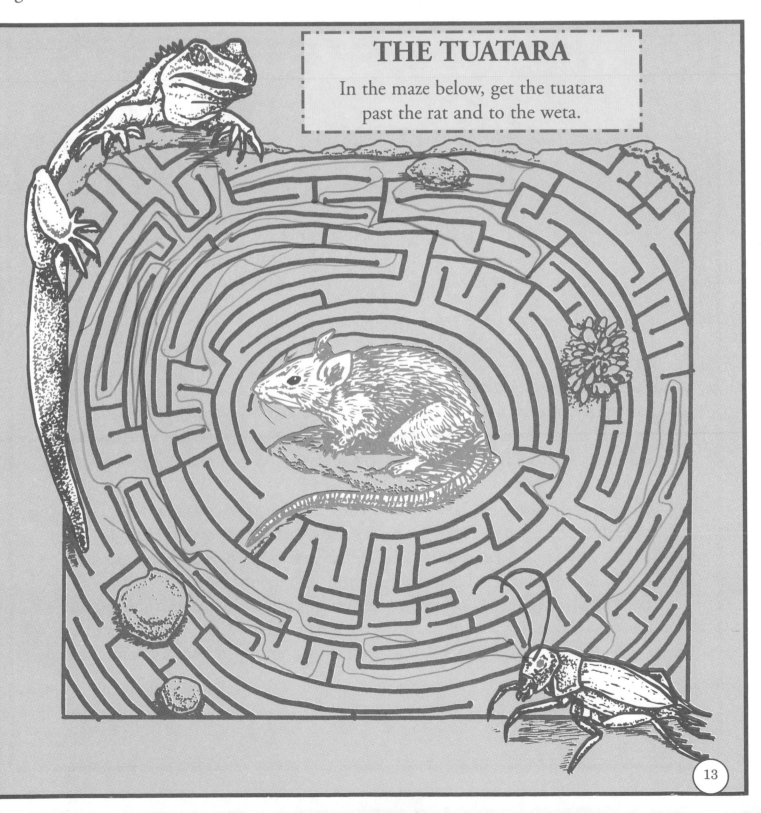

THE TUATARA

In the maze below, get the tuatara past the rat and to the weta.

All in the Family

Many creatures live in the ocean—and not all of them are fish! Whales, dolphins, and porpoises are all cousins in the cetacean *(sih-TAY-shun)* family. Cetaceans are mammals.

Like other mammals, such as humans, whales are warm-blooded. This means that a whale's body has to stay the same temperature all the time. Whales have a special coat of fat just under the skin, called blubber, which keeps them warm even in the Arctic.

Unlike fish, which get the oxygen they need right from the water, a cetacean breathes air at the water's surface through a nose in the top of its head. This nose is called a blowhole. When a whale comes to the surface and exhales, water bursts into the air in a marvelous spout.

There is another way in which whales are like other mammals. Whales give birth to live babies and then take care of them. Mother whales nurse their babies with milk, guard them against danger, play with them, and teach them.

Test your knowledge of whales and dolphins. Unscramble the underlined words below. Then fit all the words into the puzzle.

1. To keep warm, whales have **brelbub**, a special coat of fat. _____
2. Whales, dolphins, and porpoises may live in the water, but they are not **shif**. _____
3. A whale breathes air out of a **ohwolbel** on the top of its head. _____
4. Mother whales guard their babies against **regdan**. _____
5. Whales, dolphins, and porpoises are similar to **eolppe**. _____
6. Whales nurse their babies with **kiml** made in their bodies. _____
7. Mother whales **aecht** their babies, and play with them, too. _____

Bonus:
Whales, dolphins, and porpoises belong
to the **ateanecc** family. _____

DIGGING FOR DINOSAURS

Dinosaurs dominated Earth for more than 160 million years. People have been fascinated by these incredible beasts for years—ever since 1824, when the first dinosaur was named *(Megalosaurus)*.

Some dinosaurs were huge (tall enough to look into a fourth-story window), but others were no larger than a modern-day chicken. Most dinosaurs died out 65 million years ago, but some scientists believe that modern-day birds are directly related to dinosaurs.

BASIC DINOSAUR CLASSIFICATION

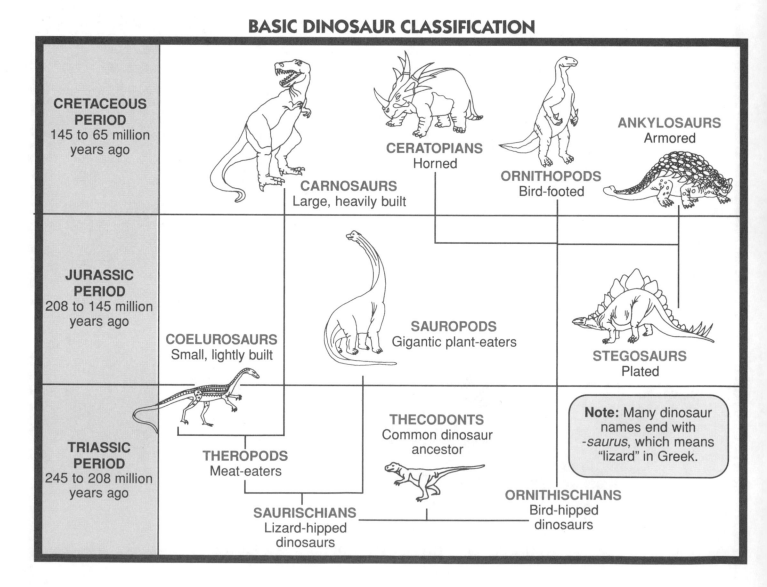

CRETACEOUS PERIOD
145 to 65 million years ago

JURASSIC PERIOD
208 to 145 million years ago

TRIASSIC PERIOD
245 to 208 million years ago

CERATOPIANS
Horned

CARNOSAURS
Large, heavily built

ORNITHOPODS
Bird-footed

ANKYLOSAURS
Armored

SAUROPODS
Gigantic plant-eaters

COELUROSAURS
Small, lightly built

STEGOSAURS
Plated

THECODONTS
Common dinosaur ancestor

THEROPODS
Meat-eaters

Note: Many dinosaur names end with *-saurus,* which means "lizard" in Greek.

SAURISCHIANS
Lizard-hipped dinosaurs

ORNITHISCHIANS
Bird-hipped dinosaurs

People have been able to learn a lot about dinosaurs by studying fossils. *Fossils* are the remains of plants or animals preserved in earth or rock. These remains can be bones, teeth, shells, footprints, or impressions of skin, feathers, or leaves. Scientists who study fossils are called paleontologists *(pay-lee-un-TAH-luh-jists)*. By studying fossils, paleontologists can find out how large a dinosaur was, where it lived, what it ate, and how it defended itself against predators.

Dinosaurs lived from 245 million years ago to 65 million years ago, during a time called the Mesozoic era. The Mesozoic era is divided into three periods: Triassic, Jurassic, and Cretaceous. The first dinosaurs appeared during the Triassic period. Frogs, turtles, crocodiles, and the first mammals also came into being during this time. During the Jurassic period, dinosaurs dominated the land. Some of the best-known dinosaurs lived during this time, such as *Stegosaurus* and *Brachiosaurus*. Dinosaurs continued to dominate during the Cretaceous period. By the end of this period, however, dinosaurs and many other animals and plants became extinct.

See if you can answer the questions below. If you have trouble, the answers are scrambled (in parentheses). To solve the mystery phrase, place the circled letters in the numbered spaces at the bottom.

1. Fossils are the remains of _____ or animals preserved in earth or rock. (S A P T L N)
2. Paleontologists are _____ who study fossils. (I E T S S I T N C S)
3. By studying fossils, paleontologists can find out _____ a dinosaur lived and how it _____ itself. (H E E R W) (D F E N E D D E)
4. The three periods of the Mesozoic era are the Triassic, Jurassic, and _____. (O E T E R S U C A C)
5. The first dinosaurs appeared during the _____ period. (I S C I A R T S)
6. Two dinosaurs that lived during the Jurassic period were Brachiosaurus and _____. (U S R O G S A S T E U)
7. Dinosaurs died out about 65 _____ years ago. (L I N L M O I)
8. By the end of the Cretaceous period, dinosaurs were _____. (T N C I E T X)

____ ____ ____ ____   ____ ____ ____ ____ ____ = _____ _____

   1   2   3   4   5   6   7   8   9

MEET THE SPIDERS!

Spiders have been on Earth for almost 400 million years. Today, there are more than 30,000 species of spiders, and scientists believe that many more are yet to be discovered. Spiders are found in almost every environment and on nearly every continent of the world.

Spiders are not insects. They belong to a group called arachnids *(uh-RAK-nidz)*. All spiders have eight legs, two body sections, and make silk. Some spiders have eight eyes. A spider also has a set of leglike structures called palps on either side of its mouth, which hold prey while it feeds. The mouth parts often include sharp fangs.

Most spiders use some type of mild venom to paralyze their prey. They capture prey in two basic ways. Web builders make sticky traps from silk, in which to capture their prey. Wandering spiders walk around hunting for prey.

garden spider

tarantula

Most common spiders, such as the black widow and the garden spider, have jaws that move from side to side. But the tarantula's jaws move up and down.

Below, unscramble the words from the spider facts above. Then solve the mystery word by placing the circled letters on the numbered lines at the bottom.

Example: k l c a b   d i w o w = b l a (c) k   w i d o w
                                              4

1- n a t u r a l a t = _ _ (_) _ (_) _ _ _ _
                           2   6

2- d e n r a g   d r i p s e = _ (_) _ _ _ _   _ _ (_) _ _ _
                                  3   7

3- r e n d w g a n i = _ _ _ (_) _ _ _ _ _
                              8

4- s p a p l = _ (_) _ _ (_)
                  1   9

black widow

5- t h i g e   s e e y = _ _ _ (_) _   _ _ _ _
                                5

MYSTERY WORD:
Spiders are _ _ _ _ _ _ _ _ _
            1 2 3 4 5 6 7 8 9

18

HELPFUL NEIGHBORS

Some people fear spiders and may even try to kill them. They don't realize that almost all spiders are helpful. Spiders eat more destructive insects than any other animal group. The garden spider keeps garden pests, such as aphids, weevils, and caterpillars, from eating and damaging vegetables and other plants.

The hungry garden spider in the maze below needs to get to its meal. But the birds are hungry for a garden spider! See if you can get the spider safely past the birds to one of its captured prey.

Home, Sweet Home

Bats have adapted to many different habitats, or environments—deserts, rain forests, and even to your own backyard. In the winter, some bats migrate, or travel, to warmer climates. The silver-haired bat flies by itself for thousands of miles to warmer climates. But other bats never travel more than 30 miles away from where they were born.

tropical fruit bat

The place where a bat sleeps is called a roost. Along the walls of a cave, a bat can grasp any little nook with its claws, and hang upside down. Other roosts include attics, bridges, large tropical leaves, trees, mines, tunnels, old buildings, abandoned termite nests, and tropical spider webs—anywhere they feel safe.

Disk-winged bats have suction cups on their thumbs and ankles. These stick to leaves when they roost. Tiny tent-building bats roost in palm leaves. These bats chew a hole in the central rib of a big palm leaf, causing the leaf to fold in half. This leaf "tent" protects the bats from rain, sun, and wind.

Some bats roost alone, or with one or two other bats. Others roost in huge colonies of thousands or millions of bats. Bracken Cave in Austin, Texas, contains as many as 20 million Mexican free-tailed bats. This is the largest known colony of warm-blooded animals in the world. Each night, the bats emerge to hunt for food. This awesome outpouring of bats can last for almost three hours!

rosette fruit bat

Bats that hibernate during the winter live on fat they stored during the summer. Their breathing slows down and their heart rate drops. During this time, they do not eat or drink. As they sleep, the combination of cool air in the cave and the warmth from the bats' bodies causes little droplets of water to form on the bats' fur. When the bats wake up, they each have instant refreshment to quench their thirst.

See if you can answer the questions below. If you have trouble, the answers are scrambled (in parentheses). As a bonus, when you have finished, put together all the circled letters and unscramble them to form a new word.

1. The silver-haired bat migrates _____. (N L O E Ⓐ)
2. When a bat sleeps for many months during the winter, this is called _____ (T N R Ⓑ E A N I O H I)
3. The place where a bat sleeps is called a ____. (O Ⓣ S R O)
4. Tent-building bats will roost in _____ leaves. (L Ⓜ P A)
5. These bats will chew a leaf in half to create a shelter. _____ (N T T E   U G D L L I I B N   S B T Ⓐ)
6. Which bat has suction cups on its thumbs and ankles? _____ (S K D I   G W Ⓝ D E I   A B T)
7. A favorite bat roost is a _____. (V A E C)
8. When a bat hibernates, it does not eat or _____. (K I D N R)
9. Bats have adapted to different _____. (I T A S T A B H)
10. The largest colony of warm-blooded animals in the world is in _____. (X A T S E)

_ _ _ _ _ _ = _____

Plenty of Penguins

Penguins are named for physical features, the people who discovered them, where they live, or their natural behaviors. It is easy to figure out why species like the rockhopper, black-footed, yellow-eyed, and chinstrap penguins were named. The emperor penguin is the largest, and the king is the second largest. The royal penguin has a white face and a golden crown of feathers, while the crested penguin has long, fancy feathers on its head. Galápagos penguins live on the Galápagos Islands, and Peruvian penguins live in Peru. Adélie penguins were named after Antactica's Adélie coast, where they live. The coast was named for the explorer's wife. Magellanic penguins were named after Ferdinand Magellan, who discovered the area where they live.

You are a scientist studying penguins, and you have to identify the different species around you. Use your knowledge of penguins and the code box below to help name them. See how many you can figure out.

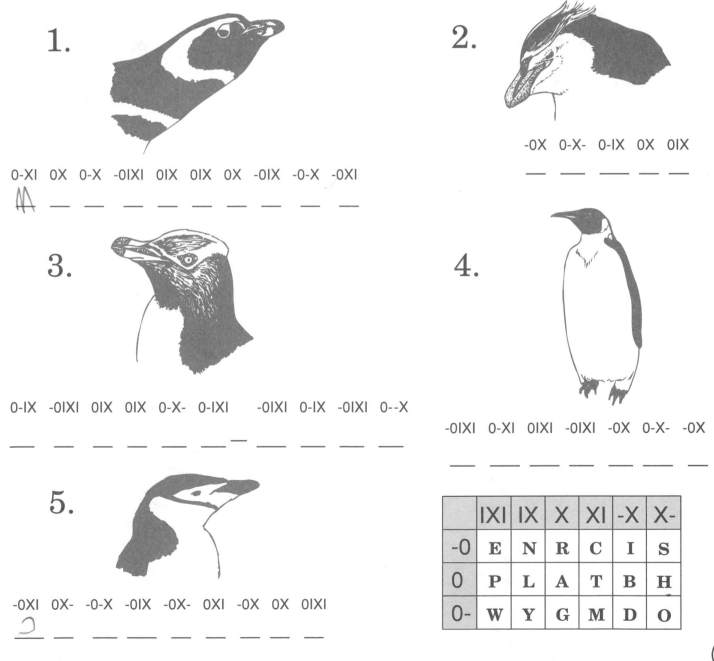

1.

0-XI OX 0-X -OIXI OIX OIX OX -OIX -0-X -OXI

2.

-OX 0-X- 0-IX OX OIX

3.

0-IX -OIXI OIX OIX 0-X- 0-IXI   -OIXI 0-IX -OIXI 0--X

4.

-OIXI 0-XI OIXI -OIXI -OX 0-X- -OX

5.

-OXI OX- -0-X -OIX -OX- OXI -OX OX OIXI

	IXI	IX	X	XI	-X	X-
-0	E	N	R	C	I	S
0	P	L	A	T	B	H
0-	W	Y	G	M	D	O

Courageous Clownfish

The little clownfish lives among the stinging tentacles of the sea anemone *(uh-NEH-muh-nee)*. The anemone looks like a plant, but is an animal, and it stings! Unlike other fish, however, the clownfish is not bothered by the anemone's sting.

Help this clownfish swim back to the wavy arms of its friend, where it will be completely safe. Be sure to avoid the predators that are looking for a quick lunch.

Duckbill Decoding

One group of Cretaceous plant-eating dinosaurs is called hadrosaurs *(HA-druh-sorz)*. They had long, wide snouts ending in broad beaks that looked something like a duck's bill. From that came their nickname: the duck-billed dinosaurs.

A duckbill's teeth were crammed into its jaws in stacks of three to five teeth one on top of the other. Up to 60 stacks and 1,200 teeth were packed into a single duckbill mouth!

There were two kinds of duckbills. Those like *Anatosaurus (uh-NAT-uh-SORE-us)* had flat heads without bony crests. The other group, which included *Lambeosaurus (LAM-bee-uh-SORE-us),* had fancy, hollow crests.

See if you can fill in the blanks below using your knowledge of duckbills. If you get stuck, decode the answer by using the code box.

1. A duckbill had up to 1,200 _____.

⨯⊤ ⋈⊢ ⋈⊢ ⨯⊤ ⨯⊩

2. Duckbills had broad _____, similar to ducks' bills.

⊠⊤ ⋈⊢ ⨯⊢ ⨯⊥ ⊠⊢

3. *Anatosaurus* had a _____ head.

⊠⊥ ⋈⊩ ⨯⊢ ⨯⊤

4. *Lambeosaurus*'s _____ were fancy, but hollow.

⨯⊤⊤ ⨯⊥⊥ ⋈⊢ ⊠⊢ ⨯⊤ ⊠⊢

5. Duckbills lived during the _____ period.

⨯⊤⊤ ⨯⊥⊥ ⋈⊢ ⨯⊤ ⨯⊢ ⨯⊤⊤ ⋈⊢ ⋈⊤ ⋈⊥ ⊠⊢

	|	⊤	⊥	||	⊥⊥	⊤⊤
⨯	a	t	k	h	r	c
⊠	s	b	f	v	y	h
⋈	e	o	u	l	i	m

Tricky Trap

The trapdoor spider is very clever. It not only builds a burrow, complete with a door, but it booby-traps the surrounding area. When a centipede, beetle, or some other prey wanders by, the trapdoor spider springs out to snag its dinner.

Despite all its defenses, the trapdoor spider lives in fear of the spider-hunting wasp. This wasp opens the lid of the burrow, dives in, and stings the spider with a paralyzing venom. The wasp then lays her eggs on the spider. When the wasp's eggs hatch, the newborn wasps feed on the living spider.

The trapdoor spider below is hungry. But the spider-hunting wasp is looking for a nesting place. Can you help the hungry spider get to its prey and avoid the wasp?

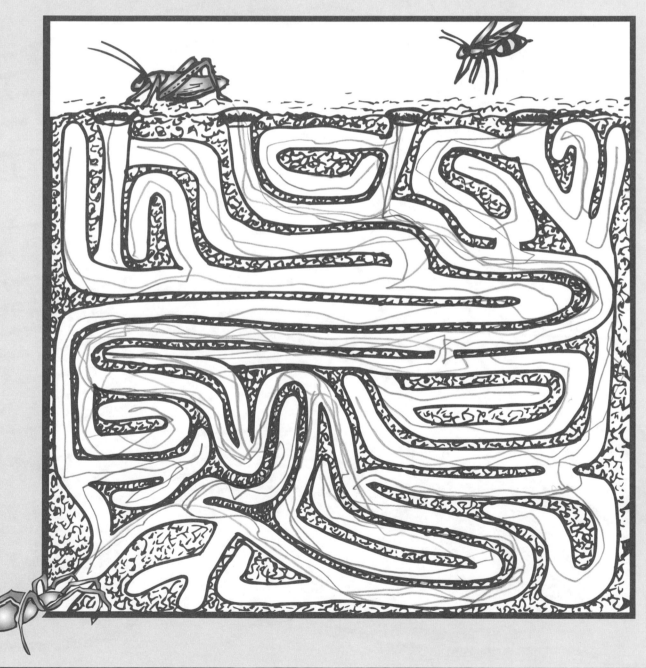

FLYING REPTILES!

There are several species of reptiles that can glide from tree to tree, or from trees to the ground. Here, the flying snake and the flying dragon are both hunting prey. But a hungry viper waits below to prey on them. Can you get the flying snake to its lizard prey? Be careful! You must watch for the viper.

Hint: The two gliding reptiles will cross paths.

Who's That Bat?

There are two basic kinds of bat: megabats and microbats. Megabats are large bats, such as the flying fox, that eat mostly fruit. Microbats, such as the free-tailed bat, are smaller bats. They eat insects and other small animals.

In this mystery picture, you will find either a fruit-eating megabat or an insect-eating microbat. To solve the puzzle, draw exactly what you see in the numbered boxes at the top into the blank boxes of the same number below.

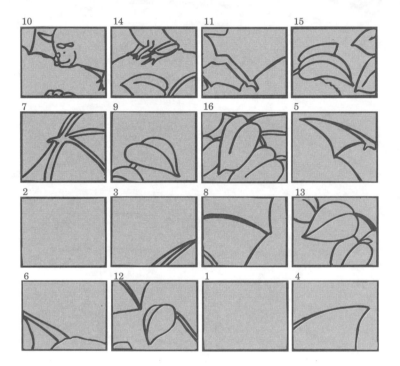

All Dressed Up

Some penguin species have similar features. The macaroni, rockhopper, royal, and erect-crested penguins all look very much alike. Scientists who study penguins can tell the difference at a glance. Can you?

Below are three each of four different kinds of penguins. Help get the identical ones together by connecting them with a line.

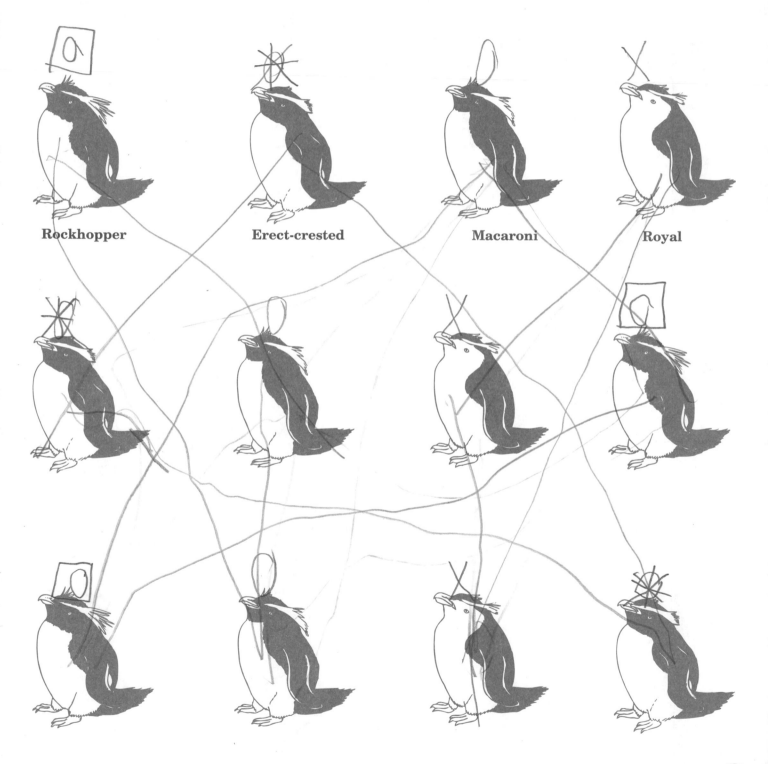

Rockhopper   Erect-crested   Macaroni   Royal

Frog Frenzy

In the picture below, you will see many types of frogs in water and marshes, and on trees. There are at least 20 frogs in the puzzle. See how many you can find. A helpful hint: Color each frog as you find it.

Big Babies

From the moment it is born, a baby whale, or calf, depends on its mother for food, protection, and the many lessons it needs to learn in order to survive. Most baby whales stay with their family group, called a pod, for at least a year, but some stay within their pod for their entire lives.

Living in a pod makes it easier to protect calves. When it is time for a whale to give birth, the females will often gather around the new mother, while male pod members may patrol the area to fend off predators.

Gray whales migrate from Alaska to Mexico to have their babies in warm lagoons. In these safe, salty lagoons, the babies easily float near the surface to breathe, and develop the thick layer of blubber they need for the trip to colder, northern waters.

Blue whale babies are 25 feet long at birth. That is as big as a small bus! The baby gets rich, fatty milk from its mother and gains hundreds of pounds each day. It can eventually grow to 100 feet and weigh as much as 30 elephants!

Identify each cetacean species shown by using the code box below. For example X · = A

	·	··	∴	∵	:
X	A	W	B	L	U	R
□	T	S	G	E	D	I
8	P	Y	O	N	H	

1. □∴ X: X· 8··
   X·· 8·· X· X∵ □∵ □··
   GRAY WHALES

2. X∴ 8∴ □· □· X∵ □∵ 8∵ 8∴ □·· □∵
   □· 8∴ X∵ 8· 8: □: 8∵ □··
   B_TTL_____ ___L___AS

3. X∴ X∵ X· □∵
   X·· 8· X· X∵ □∵ □··
   BLUE WHALES

4. □·· 8· 8∴ □· □· □∵ □·
   □· 8∴ X∵ 8· 8· □: 8∵ □··
   WP_TTRD D_LP___AS

32

Jurassic Giants

Jurassic plant-eaters included some of the biggest animals ever to walk on Earth. Lizard-hipped, plant-eating dinosaurs are called sauropods *(SORE-uh-podz). Apatosaurus (uh-PAT-uh-SORE-us)* may have weighed as much as 30 tons and measured up to 70 feet long, including its neck and tail.

The *Apatosaurus* below is hiding lots of dinosaur secrets. Use the word list to find sauropod names, behaviors, and body parts. The words go up, down, diagonally, backward, and forward.

Apatosaurus
Brachiosaurus
Diplodocus
Jurassic
long neck
planteater
sauropod
small head

SPIDER KIN

Scorpions, which are members of the spider family, are found mainly in warm regions such as Arizona and Florida, and in tropical climates. With a long tail that is used like a sword in battle, the scorpion is capable of delivering a painful and poisonous sting. The scorpion uses venom to paralyze prey and protect itself against predators. The sting of some scorpions is no more harmful to humans than a bee sting. But some scorpions, such as the small blue bark scorpion, can be deadly.

Ticks and mites are also part of the spider family. Unlike their cousins, they do not seek out prey. Instead, they are parasites, feeding on the blood of other living animals. Many mites feed on insect eggs and attack small insects that damage plants. The velvet mite is a common insect-eating arachnid.

Fill in the words missing from the sentences below.

1. Scorpions _paralze_ their prey.

2. Ticks and mites feed on _living_ animals.

3. Unlike spiders, mites and ticks do not _seek_ out prey to feed on.

4. One mite that helps keep a garden free of pesky insects is the _velvet_ mite.

5. _Ticks_ and _MITES_ are parasites.

6. Mites feed on insect _EGGS_ and protect gardens from harmful bugs.

7. Scorpions, ticks, and mites are _ARACHNIDS_

8. Some _SCORPION_ stings are harmful to humans.

9. Mites are _____ in protecting gardens from harmful intruders.

In the crossword puzzle below, fit in words missing from the sentences on page 34. Be careful! Use a pencil so you can erase mistakes. Some of the words have the same number of letters, so if your answer doesn't make sense in one place, try it in another. The puzzle has been started for you.

scorpion

bean tick

soft mammal tick

(red) velvet mite

SNAKY CROSSWORD

Snakes are amazing animals—all 2,700 known species! They live in many different habitats. Sea snakes live in a marine environment. Other snakes live in forests, deserts, and near freshwater creeks, ponds, and lakes.

Like other reptiles, snakes are covered with scales. But this armored skin does not grow with the snake, so it is shed again and again as the snake outgrows it. A snake's skin also helps it hide, because it camouflages the snake within its natural environment. A grass snake blends with green grass. The brown, patterned Gaboon viper of Africa hides easily on the forest floor. The Gaboon viper has the longest fangs of all poisonous snakes—about two inches.

With fangs, a viper can paralyze prey by injecting venom. Like other snakes, a viper uses a forked tongue as a "nose" to track down its victims. But not all snakes use fangs to kill prey. A boa constrictor uses its body to squeeze prey to death.

Snakes prey on many kinds of animals. The black mamba climbs trees to hunt baby birds. The red rat snake likes rats. The sea snake eats fish.

Test your knowledge of snakes. Fill in the words below, then complete the crossword.

Across

1. The continent that is home to the Gaboon viper is _____.
3. A marine serpent is called a _____.
5. Rat snakes hunt _____.
7. Snake skin has many _____.
9. A viper uses _____ to paralyze prey.
11. Black mambas may climb a _____ to hunt.
13. A sea snake's habitat is described as _____.
15. When the color and pattern of a snake's skin blends in with the environment, it is said to have _____.

Down

2. A boa _____ squeezes its prey to kill it.
4. Some rat snakes are _____.
6. Snakes have _____-shaped tongues.
8. _____ constrictors do not inject their prey with venom.
9. A _____ is a venomous snake.
10. A viper's venomous bite will _____ prey.
12. A snake _____ its skin.
14. Name the snake that has the longest fangs.
16. A black _____ will eat baby birds.
18. Some grass snakes are _____.

GET A LOAD OF LIZARDS

There are more lizards than any other kind of reptile—more than 3,000 species. In the word search below, there are many lizard names, as well as a few other things that have to do with lizards. The words can be found going forward, backward, up, down, and diagonally. Words in parentheses are not in the puzzle.

```
W S L S T S R R E Z A G N U S K
H N E I U D B E A R D E D M O C
I O E A Z A E G L A S S G M K D
P E T U E A S R Q U A S O D G H
T L O B G L R F A S T D O E K I
A E K A P E R D R L O S P N J L
I M A N A I T P S D L P A R M P
L A Y O L D A D R V R O M O N S
R H E L S E L A C S B U C H U T
E C E E B E G M K L E G L E S S
O D M I A O A E O I A I W N W R
A K S T N N P A O A D L G Z S O
N I C I S S R F D T E A E G R T
A M G E T M E C O D D M C A M I
U E A U G N N C Z E P O K R P N
G R P N C N W K T H K N R A T O
I R S E R U F Z F S R S E T G M
U A L L I G A T O R S T D A K H
M Z I J Y F L Y I N G E W U Z L
N K H S K I N K V T U R I T R W
```

Alligator (lizard)
Anole
Beaded (lizard)
Bearded (lizard)
Chameleons
Collared (lizard)
Fence (lizard)
Frilled (lizard)
Flying (lizard)
Gecko
Gila monster
Glass (lizard)
Horned (lizard)

Iguana
Insects
Komodo dragon
Legless (lizard)
Lizards

Monitors
Scales
Shed tail
Skink
Sungazer

Tegu
Tokay (gecko)
Tuatara
Whiptail (lizard)

EATING RIGHT

It may seem strange, but the largest whales don't have teeth. They have rows of bristled plates, called <u>baleen</u> *(buh-LEEN),* that hang from the upper jaw. Baleen is made of the same material as human hair and fingernails. Whales use their baleen to <u>strain</u> <u>plankton</u>—tiny animals and plants—from the water.

There are <u>three</u> different types of baleen whales. <u>Gray</u> whales are the only <u>bottom</u>-<u>feeding</u> great whales. They scoop sand and mud from the sea floor and force it back out through their baleen, leaving behind sea creatures such as crabs and clams to swallow.

<u>Humpback</u> whales are "<u>gulpers</u>." The <u>grooves</u> on their throats expand as they scoop up large mouthfuls of plankton-rich water or trapped fish. Then they squeeze the water out through the baleen and enjoy their dinner.

<u>Right</u> whales are "<u>skimmers</u>." They swim with their mouth partially open. The water and plankton go in the front, then the water gets forced out the sides, leaving the food in the mouth.

Make all the underlined words fit in the puzzle below. Remember, some of the words have the same number of letters as other words, so be careful.

MYSTERY SPIDER

In this mystery picture, you will find a South American spider that helps rid a valuable fruit crop of a pesky insect—the cockroach.

Draw exactly what you see in each numbered box at the top into the blank box of the same number below. When you finish your mystery picture, you can figure out the name of the spider shown by unscrambling the underlined word at the bottom.

1	2	3	4
5	6	7	8
9	10	11	12
13	14	15	16

This spider is called a <u>nabaan</u> spider.

WEB OF WORDS

Find the spidery words hidden in the web below. Words may go up, down, backward, forward, or diagonally. Some words overlap. Use this list of words to help you solve the puzzle. Words in parentheses do not appear in the puzzle.

Arachnid
Banana (spider)
Black widow
Eight eyes
Eight legs
Fangs

Garden (spider)
Hairy
Helpful
Jumping (spider)
Net casting
Orb weaver

Palps
Pest
Prey
Scorpion
Silk
Spider

Spin
Tarantula
Trapdoor
Venom
Web
Wolf (spider)

```
J O Y S J F T F N M F J N F E U O P S W Y G O K
S P I N E B J G H P P R E Y S X I G K N T Q A R
H C I H K Y L F W H I F T M Y B Y P U G R U E E
E K O U T J E T C D U P C M O P R E B M N V W D
L Y U R O M S T D Y R I A H T S M L S O A R U I
P R I H P J F I H I U V S R L P L C S E N N U P
F Y U U A I H S T G D S T S V I D Q W G I Y E S
U Y D S L B O U U R I X I O R T M B Q I O T Y C
L I G V P C Z N I G H E N V A W R M O E T R N S
L F F W S V U X T M K Y G P Y O V E W R U I V G
O T D H Y U D S V F S S B L L N K K O Q O S E E
F Y F J U D S J B I T M O P B F B W Y O T P N L
S T A R A N T U L A T N Z C V R B A N D N A L T
M O W F N W B M U D R Z D B O I E A N P I M C H
O B U E W C K I T D M P I X L N E Y G A N P W G
L D Y E E X A Y J J N T N R O A L R V R N X I I
G Z E V B O T J U I Q R H B S H C K I T B A E E
A Y D G R K D M C H M O C F H K U K O C A P T M
R F J U A J P F T B D H A H E L B C W G A I F O
D Q N K U I Z M L O P Y R F H I R E Y I F Y N L
E Y I F N W G I O E T F A N G S Z V X R D V J S
N W D G U O V B N N S G H J K L U T F T I O H E
N O G U T B C E K P E R W Q V X H Y M O R S W I
O U T J G R M V I T P V B A O T K X Z P Q O X E
```

Tigers and Leopards of the Sea

Like the wild cat it was named for, the large tiger shark has distinctive stripes on its body. The shark's stripes fade as the shark grows older. A fierce hunter of fish and sea mammals, the tiger shark is nothing like its small cousin, the leopard shark. The spotted leopard shark stays near the sea floor, searching for clams and other shellfish to grind up with its small, sharp teeth.

Get the leopard shark back to the sea floor, but avoid the tiger shark, which might just make the leopard shark its dinner!

Big Daddy

This arachnid is really a cousin to the spider. It is known by two names (one is more popular than the other). Its first name you may know by the way the spider looks. The other name was given to this arachnid because of the time of year it is most often seen.

Two of the puzzles below will reveal the name of this interesting spider. The remaining puzzles reveal characteristics that make this spider different from "true" spiders. This type of puzzle is called a rebus. Use the images shown (plus or minus some letters) to figure out what word they represent.

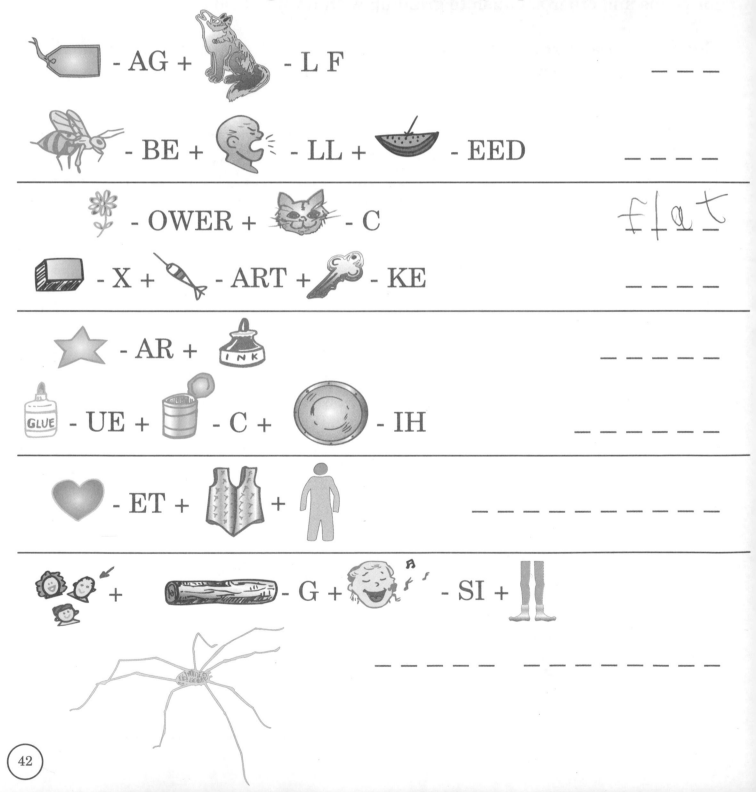

_ _ _

_ _ _ _

_f_l_a_t_ (handwritten)

_ _ _ _

_ _ _ _ _

_ _ _ _ _ _

_ _ _ _ _ _ _ _

_ _ _ _ _   _ _ _ _ _ _

42

Defenses

For whales, there is safety in numbers. Living in a pod lessens the chance that an individual will be singled out by a predator.

When a toothed whale gets into a fight with a member of its pod or with another whale species, its most common defense is to bite. However, if a small-toothed whale, such as a dolphin, is threatened by a shark, its best defense is to quickly swim away.

While size is the blue whale's main defense, it may swat an offender with its powerful flukes (tail) if surprised. Another defense for large baleen whales is breaching, or jumping out of the water and splashing back down.

The sperm whale defends itself by making a huge, explosive sound. The loud noise can stun anything that threatens the whale. Female sperm whales (cows) live in groups, which is the best defense for their babies. When threatened, the cows form a circle around the calves and face outward, ready to do battle with the predator.

Use the facts about cetacean defenses to answer the questions below. To figure out the bonus words, place each circled letter in the same numbered space at the bottom of the page.

1. Whales have many _ _ _ _(8)_ _ _ against predators.

2. A sperm whale makes an _ _ _ _ _ _ _ _ _(12) sound as a defense.

3. Toothed whales may fight by (11)_ (5)_ (7)_.

4. Dolphins may just _ _ _(10) away quickly.

5. A blue whale may swat a predator with its (3)_(9)_ _(1).

6. Female sperm whales will form a _(6)_ _ _ _ around their _ _ _ _(4)_ to protect them.

7. _ _(2)_ _(13) are safer when they live in a pod.

Bonus words: "1 2 3 4 5 Y   6 7   8 9 10 11 12 R 13"

_ _ _ _ _ _   _ _   _ _ _ _ _ _ _

1 2 3 4 5 Y   6 7   8 9 10 11 12 R 13

_

EXTRAORDINARY DEFENSE!

All reptiles have some type of defense against an attacker. Below is a scrambled picture of four reptiles and some of the ways they may defend themselves. Discover the mystery picture by drawing the image in each box in the matching numbered grid.

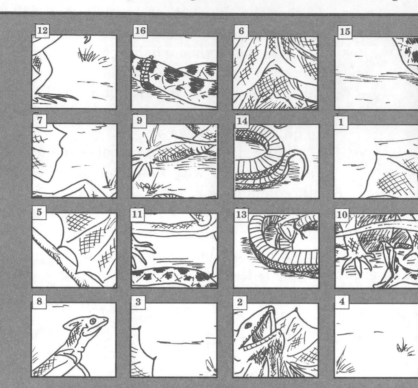

44

MORE DEFENSES

Use the code box at the bottom of the page to discover the unusual ways these reptiles protect themselves against predators.

1. The king snake looks just like a C O R A L
A5 A2 B3 B4 B1
snake, which is V E D D M O U S.
A3 C1 C2 A2 B5 A2 A6 A1
Predators stay away. This type of defense is called
I M I T A T I O N.
A4 B5 A4 C5 B4 C5 A4 A2 C2.

2. Like many lizards, the gecko can S H E D its T A I L if
A1 C7 C1 B2   C5 B4 A4 B1
a predator grabs it. The gecko gets away
and can G R O W another T A I L.
C4 B3 A2 B6   C5 B4 A4 B1

3. The gopher tortoise H I D E S in a
C7 A4 B2 C1 A1
hard S H E L L, and uses its hard, S C A L Y
A1 C7 C1 B1 B1   A1 A5 B4 B1 C3
front legs to protect its H E A D.
C7 C1 B4 B2.

4. The Gila monster is brightly C O L O R E D, which is a warning to
A5 A2 B1 A2 B3 C1 B2
predators. But the Gila's main defense is a
P O I S O N O U S bite.
C6 A2 A4 A1 A2 C2 A2 A6 A1

	1	2	3	4	5	6	7
A	S	O	V	I	C	U	B
B	L	D	R	A	M	W	Z
C	E	N	Y	G	T	P	H

People of the Trees

Apes and monkeys, like humans, belong to a group of mammals known as primates. Apes and monkeys range in size from the pygmy marmoset, just 5 inches long with an 8-inch tail, to the 350-pound gorilla. The ape family has only four members: chimpanzees, gibbons, orangutans, and gorillas. Monkeys are by far the larger family: There are 130 species.

Apes differ from monkeys in several ways. Apes lack a tail, which all monkeys have. Apes are larger than any monkey, and they walk with their knuckles on the ground. Monkeys, instead, walk on the flats of their palms.

There are at least 15 monkeys and 3 apes pictured in the forest below. Remember the differences, and see how many of each you can find.

That Famous Bat

What kind of bat appears in this mystery picture? To find out, draw the shapes from each box into the numbered blank boxes to reveal the bat's face. If you can't guess the name of the bat, unscramble the underlined words at the bottom.

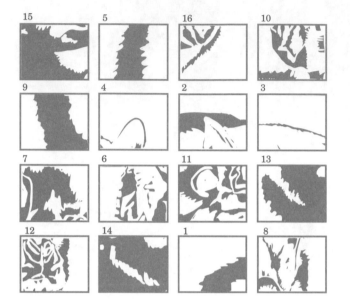

1	2	3	4
5	6	7	8
9	10	11	12
13	14	15	16

This is the famous _ _ _ _ _ _ _   _ _ _.
a p r i v e m   t b a

VARIOUS VENOMOUS SPIDERS

The four arachnids below have some of the largest fangs of all spiders. Can you identify each one? Use the chart below to decode the names. For example, if A1 is beneath the underlined space for a letter, the letter should be U.

Who is not afraid of spiders? Most spiders have sharp fangs. Spiders dangle from silk that is nearly invisible. Worst of all, spiders are venomous. The good news about spiders is that they rarely bite people. In fact, most arachnids prefer to run away from danger. They attack only when threatened, or to protect their young.

The black widow almost never leaves its web. At times, it makes its home in shoes and clothing piles. It is in places like these that the black widow is most likely to bite. Putting on your sneakers can be risky business in the southern United States. A bite from this spider can put you in a hospital with severe muscle cramps.

1) __ __ __ __ __ __ __ __ __ __
   A4 A3 B2 B4 C1 C2 C5 D2 D3 C2

2) __ __ __ __ __ __ __ __ __
   A4 D4 B2 D1 C5 A3 C5 B2 A5

   __ __ __ __ __ __ __ __ __
   C2 B2 A5 D2 C4 D4 C5 A5 C3

The violin spider is also known as the brown recluse. Usually, this spider is pretty helpful. It likes to live in loose leaves and woodpiles, and feeds on insects that may otherwise get into people's houses. But if disturbed, the violin spider is no friend. Its venom can destroy the flesh around a wound, making it ooze and burn.

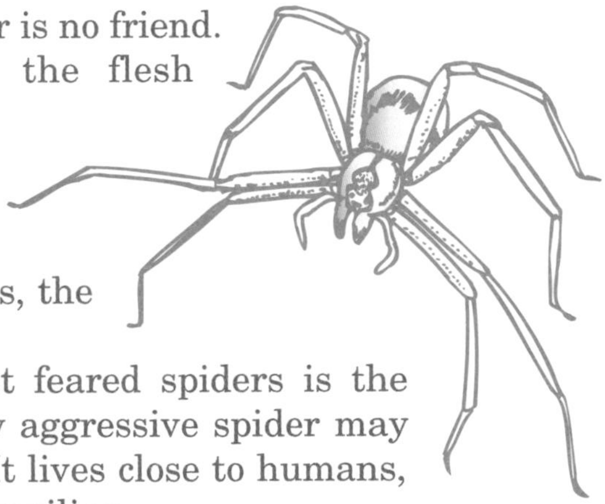

In Australia, the Sydney funnel-web spider is one of the world's deadliest spiders. This spider is very aggressive, and its poisonous bite can cause unbearable pain, convulsions, and coma. Although the bite itself is painless, the effect of the bite is terrible.

In South America, one of the most feared spiders is the Brazilian wandering spider. This very aggressive spider may bite even when there is no reason to. It lives close to humans, hiding in cupboards and closets. The Brazilian wandering spider's venom attacks the nervous system. It has been known to paralyze and even kill people.

3) __ __ __ __ __ __
   B5 C5 D3 A3 C5 A5

4) __ __ __ __ __ __
   B3 B1 D2 A5 C4 B1

   __ __ __ __ __ __ - __ __ __
   A2 A1 A5 A5 C4 A3   C2 C4 A4

	1	2	3	4	5
A	U	F	L	B	N
B	Y	A	S	C	V
C	K	W	G	E	I
D	Z	D	O	R	P

Species Pieces

Although many sea creatures have long, streamlined bodies and fins, there are big differences from species to species. Here is a chance for you to create and discover your own marine animal species. Draw or trace one of these body shapes. Then add fins, flukes, color, pattern, scales—anything you wish. Don't forget to name your new species!

Dorsal fins

dolphin

dolphin

sperm whale

orca

orca

shark

shark

second dorsal fin

fish

fish

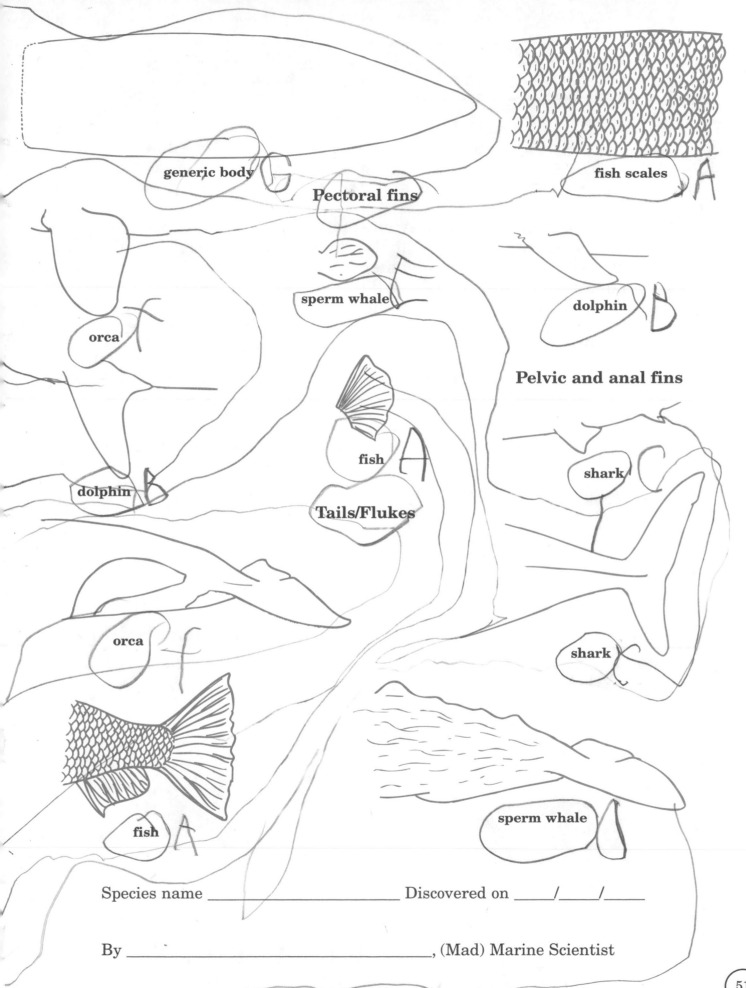

generic body

Pectoral fins

fish scales

sperm whale

orca

dolphin

dolphin

fish

Pelvic and anal fins

Tails/Flukes

shark

orca

shark

fish

sperm whale

Species name _____ Discovered on ____/____/____

By _____, (Mad) Marine Scientist

Cetaceans' Predators

Even animals as large as blue whales fear the orca, also known as the killer whale. The orca is one of the few whale species that hunts other whales. Surprisingly, the orca is gentle in captivity. Even in the wild, it does not prey on humans.

Many species of sharks will prey on small cetaceans, especially dolphin mothers with newborn babies. The mako, great white, and tiger shark will readily attack any of the smaller whale species.

One predator that won't actually kill the cetacean it preys on is the cookie-cutter shark. It swims quickly to the side of its prey, grabs it with razor-sharp teeth, and spins in a circle, removing a round chunk of flesh, which it eats.

Unscramble the words beneath each predator below to figure out its name.

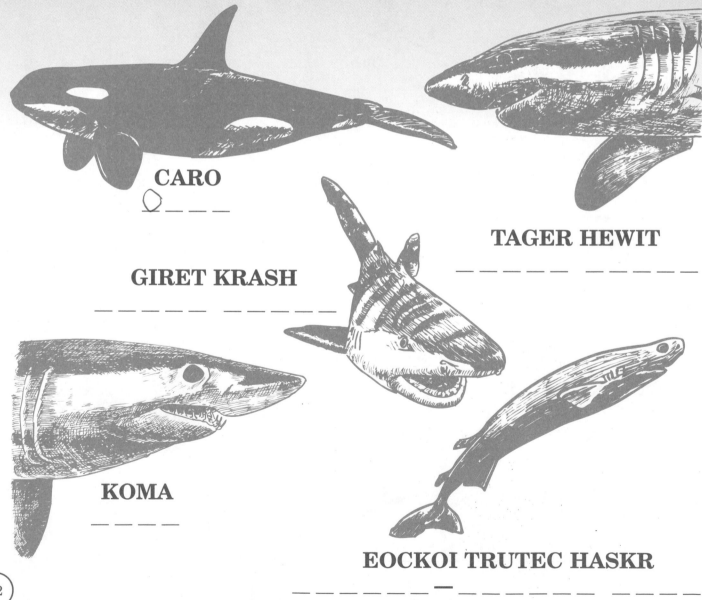

CARO

O _ _ _

GIRET KRASH

_ _ _ _ _   _ _ _ _ _

TAGER HEWIT

_ _ _ _ _   _ _ _ _ _

KOMA

_ _ _ _

EOCKOI TRUTEC HASKR

_ _ _ _ _ _   _ _ _ _ _ _   _ _ _ _ _

Crabby Family

There are more than 200 species of crab spiders in North America, and more than 3,000 species worldwide. That is a big family! Crab spiders are wandering spiders that climb flowers, then stay perfectly still while waiting for prey to come along. They got their name because, like crabs, they can walk backward, forward, and sideways, and they hold their legs outstretched at their sides. Although crab spiders do not spin webs, the female may use her silk to make a sac for her eggs. She guards the sac but dies before the babies, called spiderlings, hatch.

Crab spiders have many different colors and patterns. Can you match up each pair of identical spiders from the five pairs in the group below?

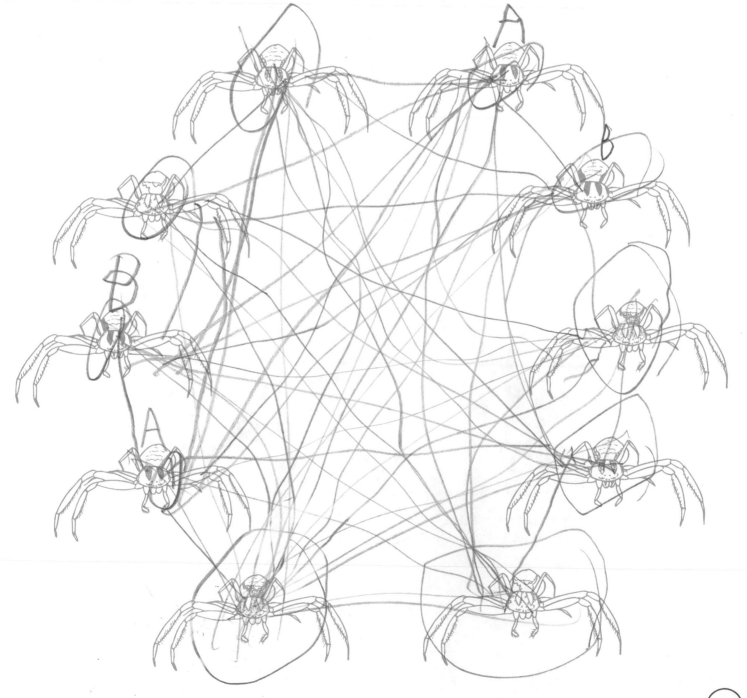

Bat Predators

There are some animals that would love to take a bat home for dinner—and not as a guest! Predators of bats include snakes, owls, hawks, cats, sun spiders, large frogs, and one bat species.

In Cuba, bat-eating boa constrictors make their homes inside caves where thousands of bats roost during the day. In the evening, when the bats emerge like a big storm cloud, boas hang from branches and grab bats that fly close by. The boas do this again in the morning, when the bats return from feeding.

In Africa, the bat hawk may occasionally feed on small birds and some insects, but bats are the main part of its diet. It has a mouth that can open wide enough to swallow little bats whole. Its eyes are huge—perfect for nighttime hunting.

Use the chart below to decode the names of some of the animals that prey on bats.

□· □· △·

_____

□· △· ◇·   □: △· △· ◇·

_____ _____

○· □· △· ○· □· □· ◇: △:

_____

◇: ○: □·· ◇· △·· △· ◇·· △: ○··
□· △· ◇·

_____

◇: □· △·   ◇: ◇· □·· ○·· △: ○·

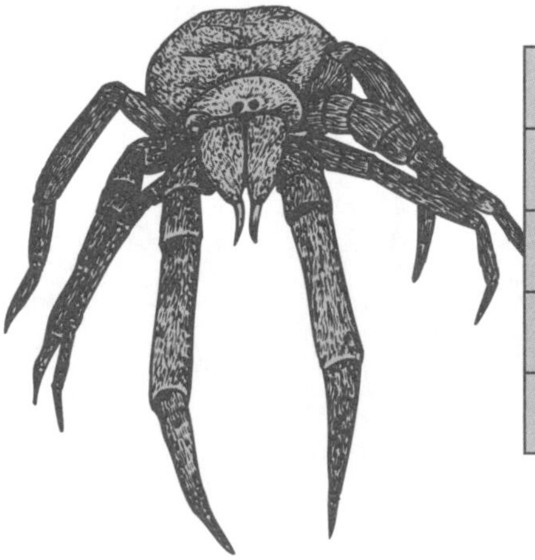

_____ _____

	·	:	··	·.	.·
□	B	H	I	U	O
△	W	E	F	N	A
◇	K	S	C	P	T
○	M	L	D	R	G

Howling Good Time!

From Alaska to Costa Rica, across Canada, and from the Pacific Coast to the Atlantic, coyotes thrive in deserts, forests, wetlands, and even cities.

Coyotes have keen eyesight, a strong sense of smell, and hearing sharp enough to detect a tiny mouse stirring under the snow. They will eat just about anything, including rodents, deer, insects, frogs, and even fruits and berries. In populated areas, a coyote will raid garbage cans and may even attack pets.

Coyotes have few natural enemies. They can survive on their own or be social and live in packs. In a pack, one dominant pair, the alpha male and female, are the only members allowed to breed. They produce litters of up to eight puppies and will stay together as a family until the pups are able to hunt for themselves. Coyotes communicate over long distances by howling, but their howl is more like a *yip-yip-yiiii* than an *arrrooo*.

Unscramble the underlined words to complete the sentences.

1. Coyotes have excellent <u>eesnss</u>. _____

2. Coyotes have few natural <u>smeenei</u>. _____

3. Coyotes can survive in <u>steserd</u>, <u>rtsfoes</u>, and <u>iitesc</u>. _____ _____ _____

4. Coyotes will eat almost <u>gyanhint</u>. _____

5. <u>closia</u> coyotes may live in <u>scpka</u>, but some coyotes live <u>enalo</u>. _____ _____ _____

6. The <u>halap</u> pair are the only pack members allowed to <u>dereb</u>. _____ _____

7. Coyote <u>trepasn</u> may have up to <u>thegi</u> <u>ipsupep</u>. _____ _____ _____

8. Coyotes <u>mucontamice</u> long <u>standesic</u> by <u>whonlig</u>. _____ _____ _____

Owl Be Seeing You

Owls are one of the few nocturnal birds, which means that they are active at night. The owl has large eyes, excellent hearing, and a head that can turn almost all the way around! Its wing feathers are frayed at the ends so that they make no noise when the owl flies. All these features make the owl an excellent hunter. Of course, a nocturnal bird of prey hunts for animals that also are nocturnal, such as rabbits, lizards, and mice.

In the maze below, a great horned owl is searching for dinner. Help the owl get to the mouse.

Eels are fish that have long, snakelike bodies. Moray eels are the best-known eel species. Moray eels have no pectoral fins, and their dorsal and tail fins are joined to form one long fin. Another species is the conger eel, which does have pectoral fins. Some snake eels have no fins at all and look a lot like sea snakes.

Using hints from the riddles below, look carefully at each eel to see if you can figure out its name. Unscramble the names to identify each eel.

1. A snake eel with a pointed tail: I S PA R T HA L
2. A moray that has links in common with a bike: H I N C A
3. It is easy to spot this moray: S T O P D E T
4. This moray could be colored by envy: E G E N R
5. This conger has a mouth full of teeth: M A D O T H E N T O Y

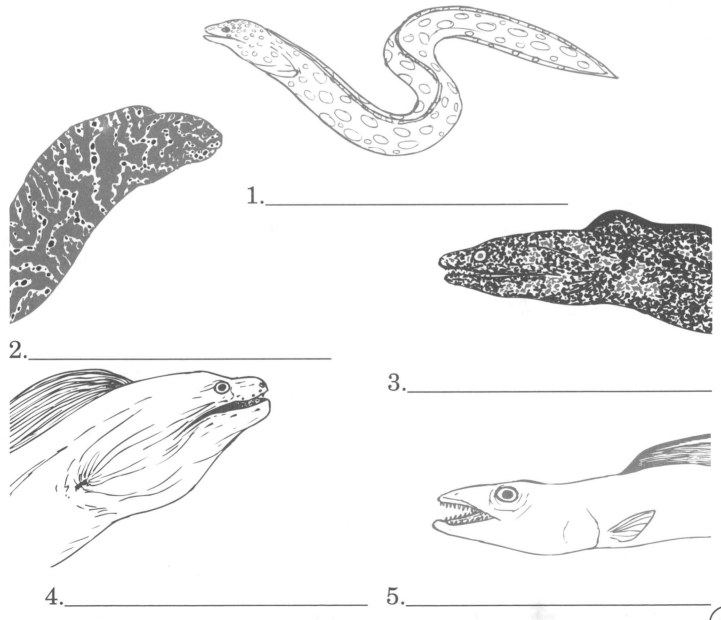

1._____

2._____

3._____

4._____   5._____

Water Sports

They might be giants, but whales are very graceful animals. Even though they may weigh many tons, whales are able to perform awesome acrobatics. They spyhop, lobtail, breach, surf, and sail.

Gray whales are known for *spyhopping*. The whale will stick its head straight up out of the water, see what is going on above the surface, sometimes spinning in a full circle, then disappear.

A *lobtailing* whale angles itself slightly downward. It raises its tail flukes into the air, then slaps them against the water's surface, making a sound as loud as a cannon shot.

To *breach,* a whale dives under water, picks up speed, then shoots straight up into the air, as high as it can. Some even leap clear out of the water! Then the whale falls back into the sea with a loud splash that can be heard for miles.

Dolphins are among the most playful of cetaceans. When a speeding boat passes by, they will race out in front and surf the bow waves, which are caused by the boat pushing through water. When racing each other, dolphins take flying leaps into the air before zipping off through the water. Dolphins also play tag, and "dance" on their tails across the water's surface.

Defenses

While bats are not very aggressive creatures, they have a number of defenses to protect themselves from predators and other dangers. One defense is to live and move in great numbers. An individual bat has a better chance of survival if it stays within a crowd of other bats.

Another defense used by bats—and many other animals—is to try to avoid danger. In fact, one of the reasons bats hunt at night in complete darkness is to avoid being seen. Some bats store food close to their roosts in places called feeding perches for nights when there is a full moon. But hunting in the dark does not protect bats from owls and bat-eating bats. Those creatures are night-hunters, too.

If bats can't avoid danger, they will try a few threat displays. A bat roosting in a person's home may feel threatened if discovered. It may growl, hiss, and bare its teeth. Usually this is enough to send a person running. If not, the bat will simply fly away.

Fighting is a last defense, but bats will show aggression when defending their territory, food supply, or mate. Some males will not allow other males to come close, and will flutter their wings and growl at them. If that fails to work, the male bats may "box" by taking swats at one another with closed wings and thumb claws.

Answer the questions below. Then use the words in the answers to fill in the crossword.

A bat has a number of defenses to protect itself from a _____ and other dangers.

Some kinds of bats move and live in great _____.

Bats hunt in complete _____ to avoid being seen by predators.

Bats may store food at _____ close to their roosts for nights when there is a full _____.

An _____ is one type of animal that preys on bats at night.

If a bat cannot escape, there are three things the bat will do when trying to scare a person or predator away: _____, hiss, and bare its teeth.

Some bat species will show _____ when trying to protect their _____, food supply, or mate.

A male bat may _____ his wings if another male comes near. If that doesn't scare off the intruder, the male bats may _____.

59

Gorilla!
How to Draw

In the forests of Africa, mountain and lowland gorillas live peacefully, having no natural enemies except humans. These shy apes live in groups, each of which consists of an adult male and several females and youngsters. The male protects the troop and leads them through their daily activities—eating plants and resting.

Gorillas, especially the mountain gorilla, are threatened with extinction. Their shrinking habitat is being cleared for farms, houses, and roads. Some gorillas are still illegally hunted for food and trophies.

Draw the mountain gorilla by following the four steps below. When you're finished, color your gorilla and draw in a lush forest setting and maybe some family members. Most of all, have fun!

1. Start by drawing the oval head and bean-shaped body. Then add the arms, legs, and feet.

2. Blend the legs and arms into the body and add the face details.

3. Sketch the edges of the fur on the legs and arms, then draw in the details of the fingers and toes. The arrows tell you which direction the fur lines will be drawn.

4. Carefully add the fur with a sharpened pencil. Note the white areas on the head and around the facial features. Leave a little sparkle in the eyes.

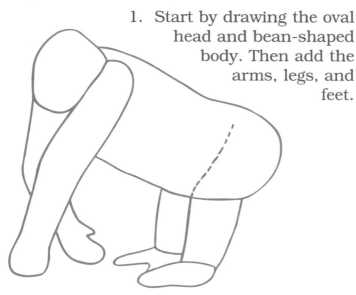

On The Fly On The Fly On The Fly

Many types of insects can fly. Flight allows insects to look for food, escape from predators, and even communicate with one another. Some insects have wings that are clearly visible. Other insects keep their wings tucked under leathery covers, opening them only when they are ready to take off.

Some insects have wings for only a short period of their lives. Certain members of ant and termite colonies grow wings in order to fly off and start new colonies. Then the wings drop off.

Using the code box below, see if you can identify these species of winged insects.

1. $\overline{ç∞}$ $\overline{∫¢}$ $\overline{∫@}$ $\overline{∫@}$ $\overline{å¡}$ $\overline{ç∞}$

   $\overline{∫@}$ $\overline{ç¡}$ $\overline{å@}$ $\overline{å¢}$

   $\overline{å∞}$ $\overline{ç¡}$ $\overline{ç¡}$ $\overline{å£}$ $\overline{∫@}$ $\overline{ç¡}$

2. $\overline{∫¡}$ $\overline{å¡}$ $\overline{∂¡}$ $\overline{å¢}$ $\overline{å@}$ $\overline{∫£}$ $\overline{ç¡}$

3. $\overline{∂¡}$ $\overline{ç¢}$ $\overline{ç¡}$ $\overline{ç¡}$ $\overline{ç@}$

   $\overline{∫¡}$ $\overline{å@}$ $\overline{ç¢}$ $\overline{ç@}$ $\overline{ç¡}$ $\overline{ç¢}$

4. $\overline{∂∞}$ $\overline{å¡}$ $\overline{ç@}$ $\overline{ç¡}$ $\overline{∂@}$

   $\overline{å∞}$ $\overline{ç¡}$ $\overline{ç¡}$

	¡	@	£	¢	∞
å	O	A	T	F	B
∫	D	L	C	I	S
ç	E	N	Z	R	W
∂	G	Y	P	U	H

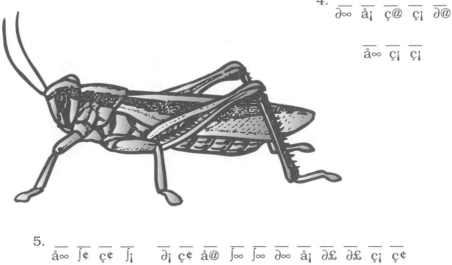

5. $\overline{å∞}$ $\overline{∫¢}$ $\overline{ç¢}$ $\overline{∫¡}$ $\overline{∂¡}$ $\overline{ç¢}$ $\overline{å@}$ $\overline{∫∞}$ $\overline{∫∞}$ $\overline{∂∞}$ $\overline{å¡}$ $\overline{∂£}$ $\overline{∂£}$ $\overline{ç¡}$ $\overline{ç¢}$

SHOCKERS & STINGERS

The ocean's residents have unique ways of hunting prey and defending themselves. Sea snakes, cousins to land snakes, have developed paddlelike tails for life in the water. Many fish and rays have sharp stingers coated with a venomous slime, and the torpedo ray has an electric charge that is so strong, it could knock a person backwards! Some jellyfish, sea wasps, and even corals can sting a human badly enough to require medical attention.

In the word search below are names and behaviors of some shocking and stinging sea creatures. Using the word list at left for help, see how many you can find. They are hiding up, down, backward, forward, and diagonally. Words in parentheses are not in the puzzle.

barb
bite
box fire coral
electric ray
fire coral
fire sponge
fireworm
hydroid
jellyfish
lionfish
man-o'-war
moon jelly
poison
scorpionfish
sea snake
sea wasp
stargazer
stingray
sun anemone
torpedo ray
touch-me-not sponge
venom

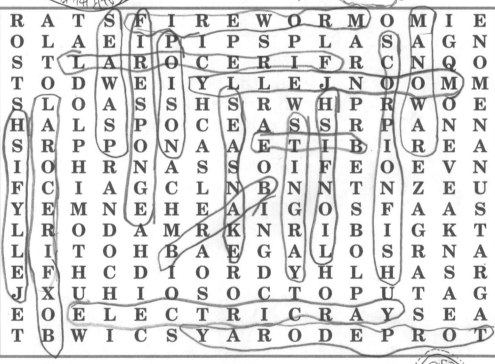

```
R A T S F I R E W O R M O M I E
O L A E I P I P S P L A S A G Q E N
S T L A R O C E R I F R C N Q N O
T O D W A I S Y L L E J N O O M O M
S L O W A S S I H S R W H P R W O N E
H A L P S P O N A C A E T I B I A N E
I R O P R A N G E A S S O N T P O N N A
F C I M O D A H B A E G R H O F I N U
Y E R O A M R N G R A B S I S T
L R F H C D I O R D Y H L H A T A R G
E I X U H I O S O C T O P U T A S A T G A
J O E L E C T R I C R A Y S E A
T B W I C S Y A R O D E P R O T
```

Butterfly Bats

The butterfly bat is a native of Africa. Named for the way it flies, the bat has wings that resemble a butterfly's. Some butterfly bats have patches of different colored fur, to blend in with the environment. Butterfly bats live in palm fronds and near banana trees, where they can feed on small insects.

Each of the butterfly bats below has a twin. Try to match them up!

Can You Bear It?

There are eight bear species. They can be found in Asia, North America, South America, and Europe.

Brown bears are the most numerous and have the greatest range. Polar bears live only near the Arctic ice cap. The black bear of North America ranges from Canada to Mexico, and its cousin, the Asiatic black bear, lives in forests throughout Asia. The sloth bear lives on the Indian subcontinent. The only bear of South America, the spectacled bear, gets its name from its facial markings. The smallest, weighing only about 100 pounds, is the sun bear of southeast Asia. The rarest bear is the giant panda. In the wild, it lives only in China, in an area just 300 miles long and about 80 miles wide.

Use the code box below to identify each of the five bear species shown.

	ø	◊	¬	•	≈	π
ß	Y	E	N	K	R	C
√	H	P	A	W	M	T
µ	D	O	J	G	V	I
≥	L	B	Z	S	F	U

1. $\overline{µ•}$ $\overline{µπ}$ $\overline{√¬}$ $\overline{ß¬}$ $\overline{√π}$
   $\overline{√◊}$ $\overline{√¬}$ $\overline{ß¬}$ $\overline{µø}$ $\overline{√¬}$

2. $\overline{≥•}$ $\overline{√◊}$ $\overline{ß◊}$ $\overline{ßπ}$ $\overline{√π}$ $\overline{√¬}$ $\overline{ßπ}$ $\overline{≥ø}$ $\overline{ß◊}$ $\overline{µø}$

3. $\overline{≥◊}$ $\overline{≥ø}$ $\overline{√¬}$ $\overline{ßπ}$ $\overline{ß•}$

4. $\overline{µ•}$ $\overline{ß≈}$ $\overline{µπ}$ $\overline{≥¬}$ $\overline{≥¬}$ $\overline{≥ø}$ $\overline{ßø}$

5. $\overline{≥•}$ $\overline{≥π}$ $\overline{ß¬}$

WEB WIZ

A spider web may look fragile, but it's an amazing tool that spiders use to hunt prey. Some webs can be three times stronger than a steel thread! The stickiness of the silk, combined with its enormous strength, practically guarantees that an insect caught in the web will not escape.

The web also alerts the spider to the presence of prey by sending vibrations through the silk. Orb web weavers, such as the golden silk spider, have poor eyesight. Vibrations on the web tell them the size and location of prey snared in their traps.

Follow the steps taken by the orb web weaver to create your own web below.

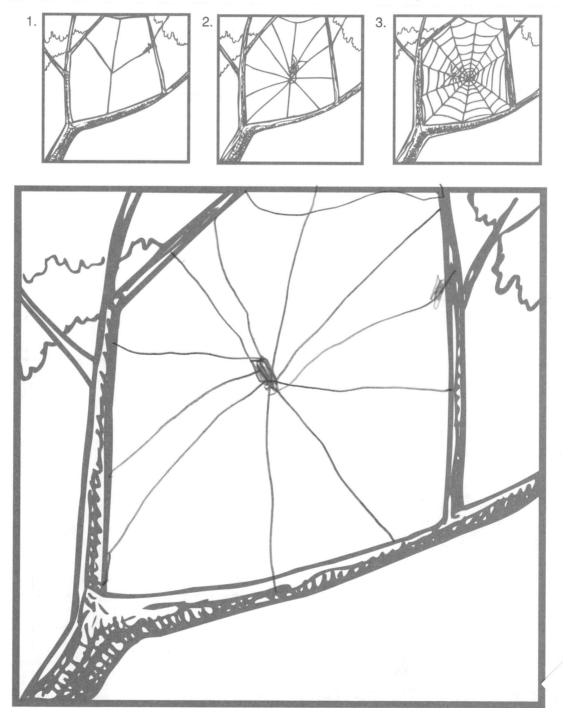

Silent Hunters

All cats are born hunters. From the 600-pound Siberian tiger to a pet kitty, cats possess the skills needed for silently stalking and pouncing on prey. Some cats sneak up close, then chase down prey. Lynxes have very long legs that enable them to chase snowshoe hares through snow.

A cat's coat is suited to its habitat. Lions rely on their tawny coats to blend in with the brush on the African plains. Tigers live in forests, so their striped fur blends in with streaks of light coming through the trees and tall grasses. Some cats, such as the ocelot and margay, have spotted or dappled coats and make their homes in trees. The caracal's golden coat blends with the tall grasses on the African plains. When a bird flies low looking for a meal, the camouflaged caracal leaps and swats the bird right out of the air!

Use the clues to find the correct answers for the crossword.

Across

2. Environment
3. Lynx prey
4. What cats hunt
5. Cats _____ prey
8. Largest of cats
11. Long-legged cat
12. Cats that live on the plains of Africa

Down

1. Sneak up close and _____ down prey
2. Born _____
4. Lion habitat
6. Pet _____
7. Leaping cat
9. Tree cat
10. Tiger habitat

DEEP MYSTERY

In the grid below is a mixed-up whale. It needs your help to get back together. Draw exactly what you see in each box on the left into the blank box with the same number on the right. Once you have completed the picture, see if you can unscramble the words below to identify the name of the whale. Then see if you can tell what this whale is doing.

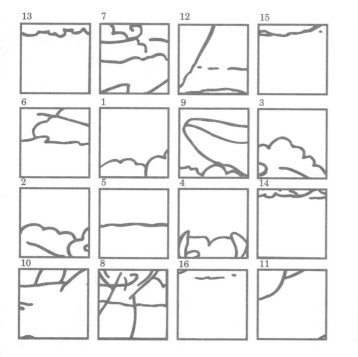

AGYR HEAWL

The whale is a _ _ _ _   _ _ _ _ _ .

Forest Spirits

Wolves live in family groups, called packs, of 6 to 15 members. The pack leaders are the alpha male and female. Wolves communicate by howling, and their ancient song can be heard for miles. Pack members keep track of one another, and any strange wolves in their territory, by howling.

In the maze below, the alpha male and female have become separated from the rest of their family. Help them find their way back to their pups.

Meet the Beetles!

There are more than 300,000 species of beetles—more kinds than any other animal in the world. Some can be six inches long and have massive jaws or horns. Some only crawl, some fly, some swim, and some bore into wood and plants. It seems like there is a beetle for every occasion!

With all those beetle species, it may be hard to tell one kind from another. The five pairs of beetles below look very much alike. Can you match each beetle with its identical twin?

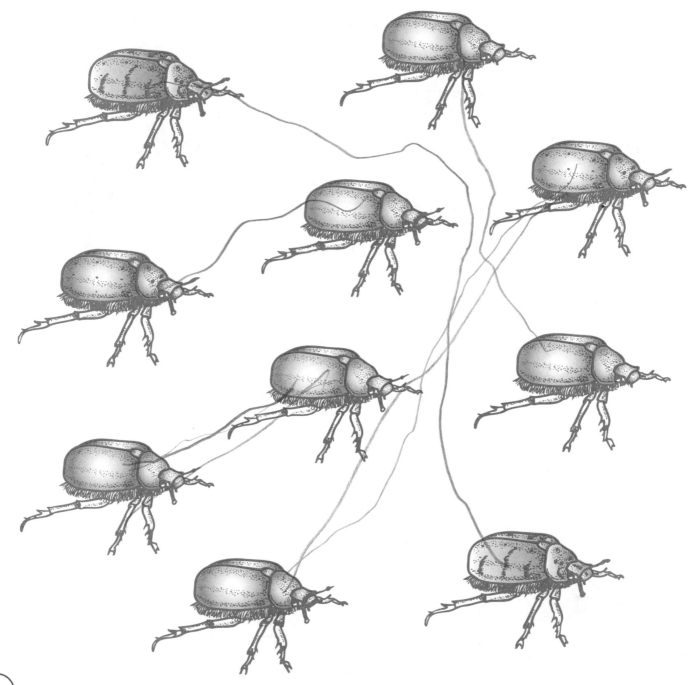

On Porpoise

The word *porpoise* comes from the Latin words for "pig fish." There are six species of porpoises, and they all look and act differently from one another.

The fast-swimming Dall's porpoise can skim through the sea at speeds of up to 45 miles per hour. Sometimes these porpoises travel in pods of up to 1,000 members.

Vaquitas are the smallest of all porpoises. Like other porpoises, they live closer to shore than dolphins, and easily fall victim to fishing nets. Only a few hundred of the endangered vaquitas remain in the wild.

Instead of a dorsal (back) fin, the finless porpoise has a ridge that runs down its back. Finless porpoise babies can often be seen hitching a ride on their mother's back, coming all the way out of the water when she comes up to take a breath.

Complete the sentences below. Then fit the underlined words into the puzzle.

Across

3. There are only six species of _____ in the sea.
4. Finless porpoise _____ hitch a ride on their mother's back.
7. The _____ is the smallest porpoise.
8. The _____ porpoise has no dorsal fin.

Down

1. Porpoises _____ and act differently from one another.
2. The Dall's porpoise is a very fast _____.
5. The word *porpoise* is Latin for _____.
6. The _____ porpoise sometimes travels in groups of as many as 1,000.

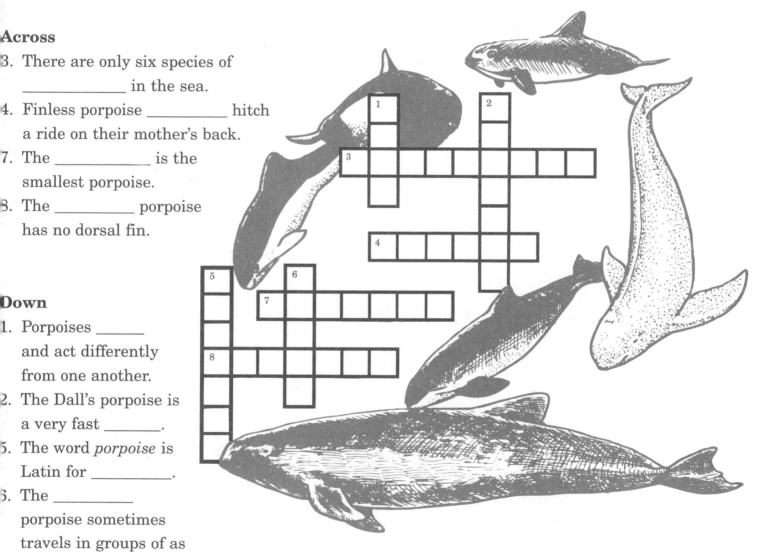

Fly-Fishing

While most bat species feed on insects, some prefer to hunt other kinds of prey. The fishing bat roosts in trees close to ponds so it can watch the water's surface for ripples caused by fish. Then it swoops in with its long toes and sharp claws and snatches the fish. The fishing bat doesn't like to eat and run, though. It stuffs the fish into its large cheeks to eat later. This fishing expert can catch as many as 40 fish in one night.

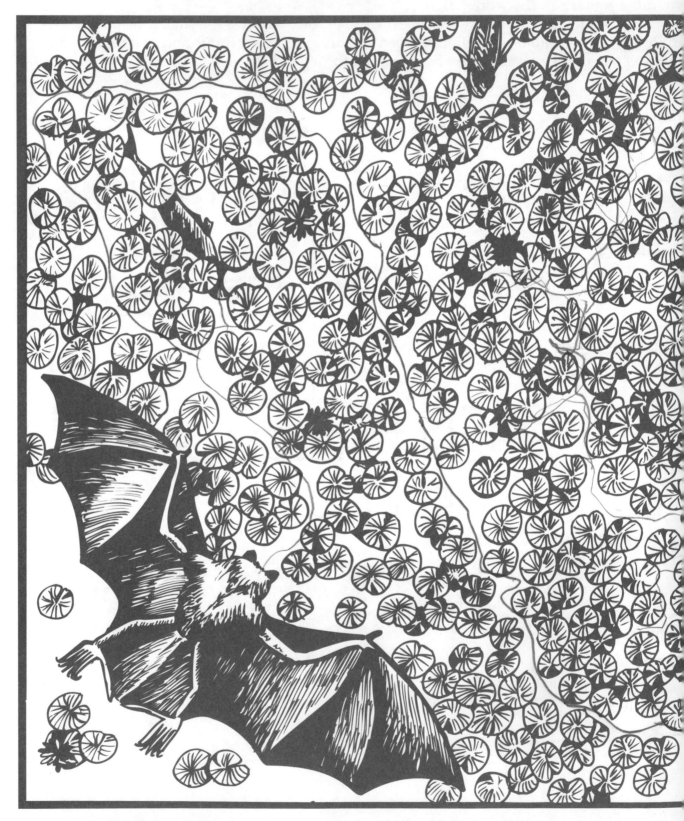

In the maze below, a fishing bat is hunting fish that are hiding among the lily pads. Can you help the fishing bat get to its prey, yet avoid getting eaten by its archenemy, the bat-eating owl? The bat in this maze will be able to reach only one fish.

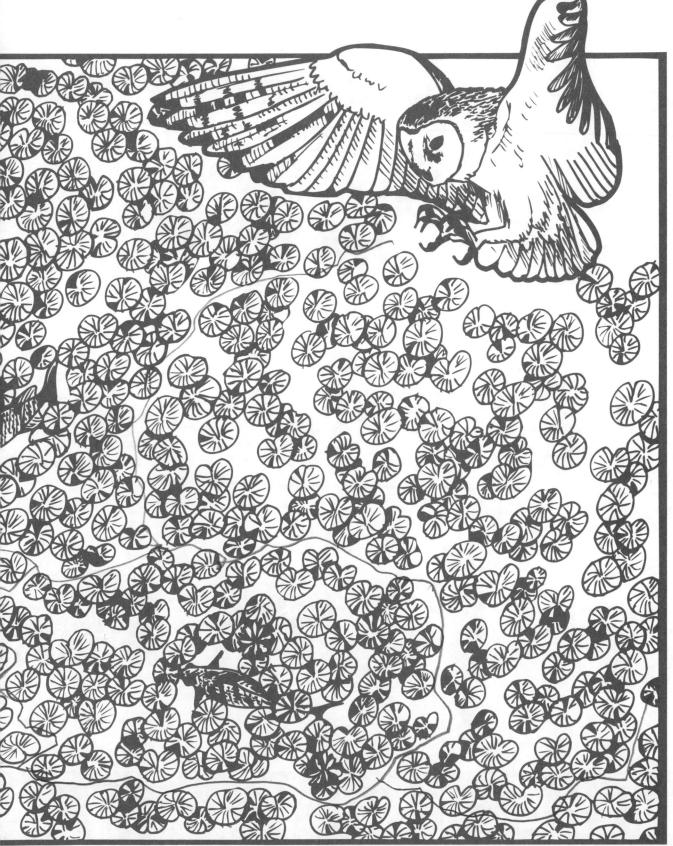

Tortoises live on land, and turtles live in the water. Turtles that live in freshwater ponds are sometimes called terrapins. There are almost 300 species of turtles and tortoises in all. Most are covered with a shell that has scales, or plates.

Solve the picture puzzle below, to identify the three turtles pictured.

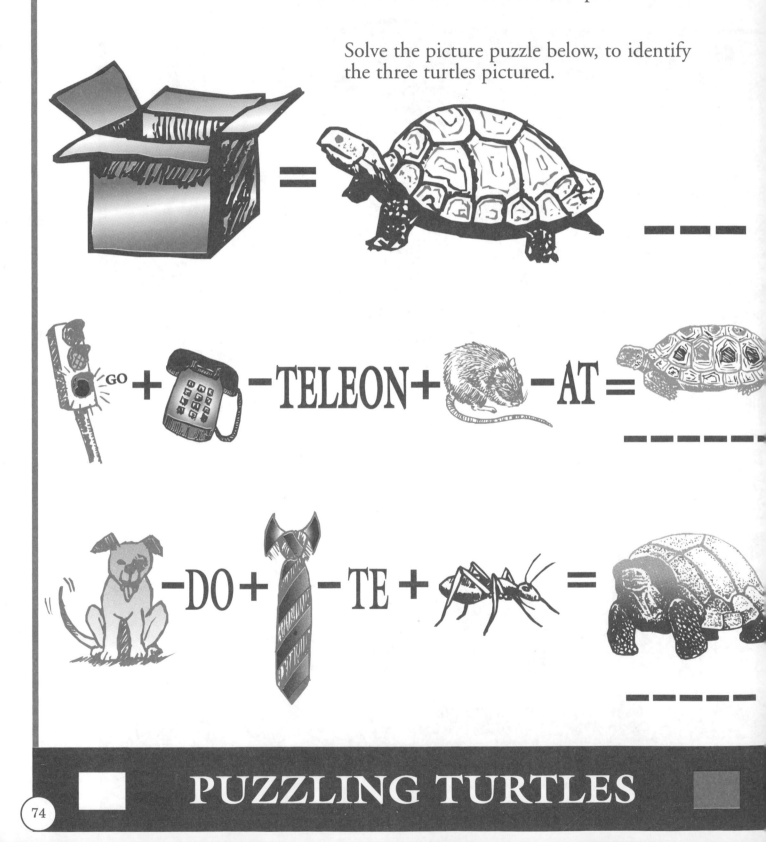

IT'S A SNAP!

In this mystery picture, you will find the alligator snapping turtle, one of the world's largest freshwater predators. But you must draw it to solve the puzzle. Look at the numbered picture boxes. They are all scrambled. Draw each picture in the blank box with the same number.

Tails of the Deep

It is hard to imagine, but some whale and dolphin species can zip through the water as fast as a speeding car! The two sides of their powerful tail, called flukes, enable them to do this. Also, with the help of their dorsal fins and flippers, whales and dolphins can steer their way through the water.

Whales use their flippers to steer, to slow down, and sometimes to knock away an attacker. The humpback whale's flippers are sometimes one third the length of its entire 50-foot-long body (which would make their flippers more than 15 feet long!).

Some whales have very large heads compared to the rest of their bodies. Their necks are stiff, to keep their large heads steady while swimming. For this reason, most whales cannot turn their heads from side to side.

On tracing paper, create your own whale species, using the shapes below.

Heads

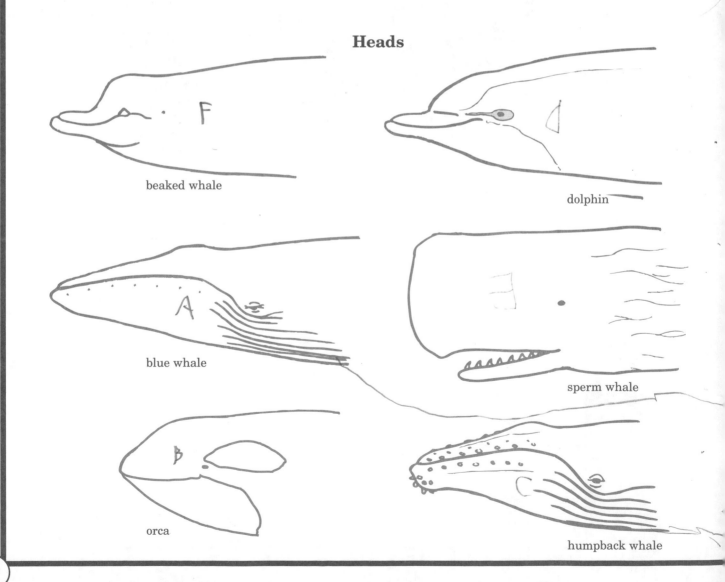

beaked whale

dolphin

blue whale

sperm whale

orca

humpback whale

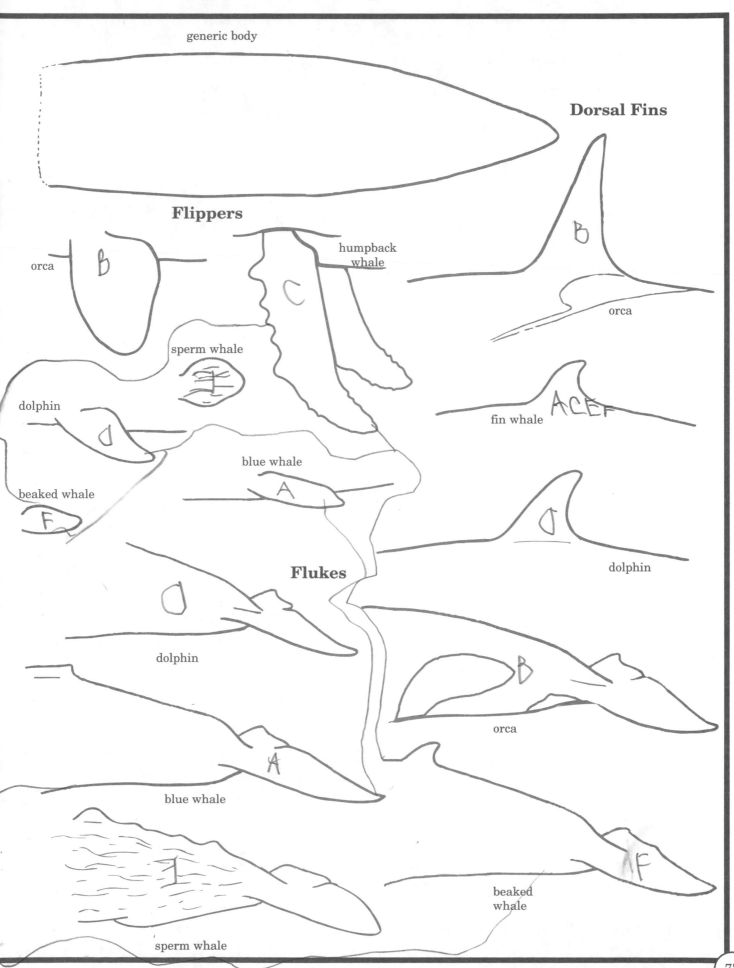

generic body

Dorsal Fins

Flippers

orca B

humpback whale

C

sperm whale

orca

dolphin

fin whale ACEF

beaked whale F

blue whale A

dolphin G

Flukes

dolphin

dolphin

orca B

blue whale A

sperm whale I

beaked whale F

Hairy Hunters

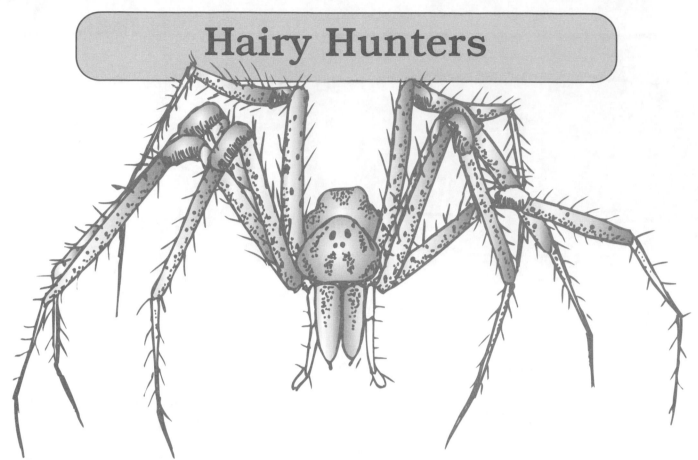

Spiders use different methods to hunt and catch prey. Some spiders chase prey, while others wait for prey to come to them. Some use webs. Others use camouflage. There are even a few spiders that spit poison or sticky fluid from their fangs to catch prey. By using different methods of hunting, spiders of different species may live in the same general area without competing with each other. This also means that one spider may end up as another spider's dinner!

Most wandering spiders do not build webs or burrows. Like wolf and huntsman spiders, they prefer to stalk, chase, and pounce on prey.

Fishing spiders feed on fish and other small aquatic animals. Some fishing spiders live under water in a silk tent, or sac. As a fishing spider dives under water, air bubbles collect on its abdomen. When the spider goes inside the sac, air bubbles fill the sac, giving the spider an airtight home in which to live and breathe under water.

The female green lynx spider and the spitting spider have an unusual way of handling prey. The female green lynx spider can shoot streams of stinging venom at prey up to eight inches away. The spitting spider spits sticky fluid, pinning its prey with a liquid net.

The purse-web spider builds a burrow lined with silk, similar to that of the trapdoor spider. But instead of a lid, the purse-web weaves a hollow sac, like the finger of a glove, that lies on the ground outside the burrow. The spider hides inside this "purse," waiting for prey to crawl over the web. When this happens, the purse-web spider rips open its sac and snatches its prey.

Unscramble the underlined words below, then fit them into the crossword.
Two words have been done for you.

1. Some spiders <u>seach</u> their <u>rype</u>. (9) <u>chase</u> (10) <u>prey</u>
2. The <u>uepsr</u> <u>ewb</u> spider digs a <u>rowrub</u> and weaves a silk sac in which it waits for prey.
   (7) _____   (8) _____   (11) _____
3. The <u>regne</u> <u>xyln</u> spider spits <u>moven</u> at its prey.
   (5) _____   (6) _____   (2) _____
4. Some <u>shingif</u> spiders can survive <u>druen</u> the
   <u>trawe</u>. (3) _____   (12) _____   (13) _____
5. Most <u>flow</u> and <u>stannhum</u> spiders do
   not build webs. (1) _____   (4) _____

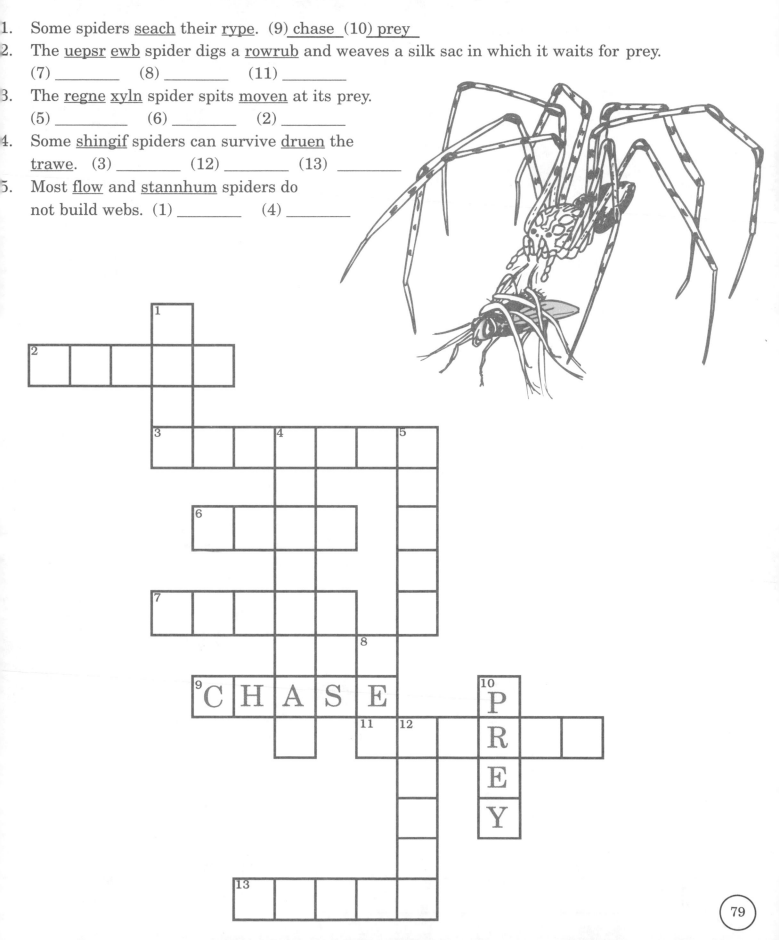

CROCODILE SMILES

Crocodiles are among the largest and most ferocious of the reptiles. These reptiles have very recognizable snouts. Can you identify the ones pictured here? Use the chart below to decode their names.

ABOUT CROCODILES

Outdone in length only by the python and anaconda, the Indo-Pacific crocodile is the largest and most feared reptile living today. Also known as the saltwater crocodile, it weighs in at more than 2,200 pounds and can grow to 23 feet!

The Nile crocodile grows to 18 feet and is considered a man-eater. It lives in freshwater rivers of central and coastal Africa. A large Nile crocodile can take down very large game animals, such as water buffalo and zebra. But it can live peacefully alongside the equally aggressive hippopotamus.

In the United States, the American crocodile is an endangered species. This 15-foot crocodile is found in the Florida Everglades and throughout the Caribbean and Cayman Islands. Although the American crocodile is not particularly aggressive, it is still considered dangerous.

The very rare Siamese crocodile, now raised on farms, may be extinct in the wild. This little crocodile is only about 13 feet long.

① __ __ __ __
  B2 C4 B4 B5

__ __ __ __ __ __ __
C1 C3 C2 B2 B3 B2 C2

② N I L E
  C4 B2 A2 A3

③ S I A M E S E
  A1 B2 C3 C5 A3 A1 A3

④ A M E R I C A N
  C3 C5 A3 B1 B2 C2 C3 C4

	1	2	3	4	5
A	S	L	E	T	W
B	R	I	F	D	O
C	P	C	A	N	M

80

ALLIGATOR ALLEY

The American alligator is legendary. Through the southern United States, it has been the subject of songs and folk tales. At one time, American alligators were being killed for their skin. But laws were passed to protect adult alligators and their eggs. The laws worked. Today the once-endangered American alligator is again thriving.

In Florida, many alligators can be seen. To some people, all alligators look alike. But just like any animal, each alligator has certain unique marks or characteristics. Test your skills of observation in this puzzle. Below are six alligators, and each one has a twin. Can you match them up?

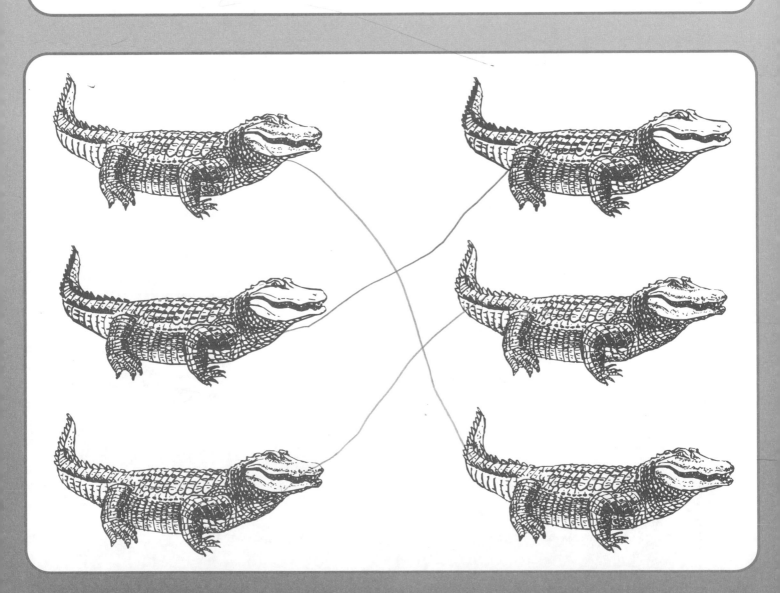

Dinosaur Roundup!

In the picture below, you will see many types of dinosaurs from all eras. There are at least 20 dinosaurs and other prehistoric reptiles in the puzzle. See how many you can find. A helpful hint: Color each dinosaur as you find it.

Penguin Crossword

Penguins live only in the Southern Hemisphere, from the Galápagos Islands, near the equator, to the continent of Antarctica. Icy currents there provide all the foods penguins hunt, such as plankton, squid, and small fish.

There are 17 kinds of penguins, varying in size from the 18-inch-tall fairy penguin to the emperor penguin, which stands over 3 feet tall. Penguins can't fly with their flipperlike wings, but they can swim faster than some birds can fly!

During breeding season, many penguins form a large colony called a *rookery* where they lay their eggs. Each female penguin only lays one egg. Some penguins build nests in the rookery. Others, such as the emperor penguin, keep the newly laid egg warm by holding it on their feet, covered by their fat bellies. This keeps the eggs warm enough to hatch, even at 40°F below zero.

Across
4. Baby penguins come from _____ .
6. Penguin food
8. Cold continent
9. Penguin colony
11. The smallest penguin
12. Penguin food

Down
1. Penguins _____, not fly
2. Earth's "waist"
3. The largest penguin
5. Penguins live in the _____ Hemisphere.
7. Not cold
10. Penguin food
11. Some penguins hold eggs on their _____.
13. What eggs need to do

Bat Bits

In this word search puzzle, see if you can find behaviors, physical characteristics, and other "batty" words listed below. Remember that the words may go up, down, backward, forward, or diagonally.

Blood
Crest
Echolocation
Flying
Fruit
Fur
Growl
Hibernation
Insect
Mammal
Megabat
Microbat
Migration

Nectar
Nose leaf
Nostrils
Nurse
Roost
Scent glands
Sword nose
Tail
Thumb
Ultrasound
Warm-blooded
Wing

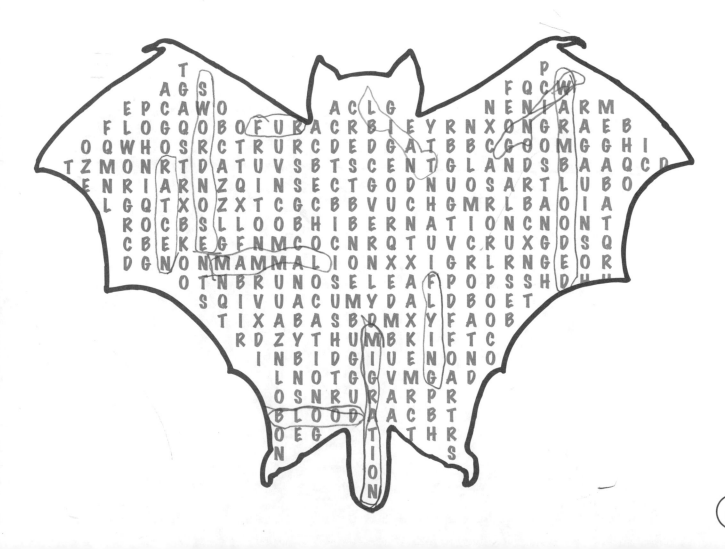

DEEP DIVERS

The sperm whale is the largest toothed whale. A 60-foot-long male sperm whale is the deep-diving champion of all the cetaceans. To hunt for its favorite prey, the giant squid, a sperm whale can hold its breath for more than one hour and dive to depths of almost two miles.

The giant squid is a frightful opponent, also growing to 60 feet or longer. It has a sharp, parrotlike beak, and has hooks inside the suction cups of its long, strong tentacles. Many sperm whales have large scars made by the giant squid's powerful suckers.

In the maze below, a sperm whale is hunting for giant squid in the ocean depths. Help the whale find one.

Raptors

Velociraptor, Utahraptor, and *Oviraptor* are all better known as "raptors." *Velociraptor* is a well-named dinosaur. The name of this man-sized predator means "swift thief," and this animal was built for speed, with a light-boned body and long, sturdy legs. It also was built for catching and killing prey: Its hands and feet ended in big, sharp claws.

Utahraptor has been called one of the most intelligent—and vicious—of all dinosaurs. Its toe claw may have been more than 15 inches long.

Oviraptor means "egg thief," because the first *Oviraptor* fossil found (in the 1920s) was on top of eggs thought to belong to *Protoceratops*. But in 1993, an *Oviraptor* embryo was found inside an egg of the same type! The fossil turned out to be a mother *Oviraptor* with her own eggs.

Based on what you have read above, can you unscramble the raptor-related words below?

1. HIGTL-NBOED DBYO _ _ _ _ _ _-_ _ _ _ _ _ _ _ _ _

2. HRAPS WSACL _ _ _ _ _ _ _ _ _ _

3. OLGN GESL _ _ _ _ _ _ _ _ _

4. GESG _ _ _ _ _

5. TWFSI IHFET _ _ _ _ _ _ _ _ _ _

6. DAREPTRO _ _ _ _ _ _ _ _ _

7. ROPTARCILEOV _ _ _ _ _ _ _ _ _ _ _ _

8. GEG FHETI _ _ _ _ _ _ _ _

9. THATRUARPO _ _ _ _ _ _ _ _ _ _

10. RTPRAOOVI _ _ _ _ _ _ _ _ _

CATCH OF THE DAY

The largest sharks in the world are the basking shark, the megamouth shark, and the whale shark. These harmless animals have tiny teeth that are no more dangerous than rough sandpaper. They feed mainly on plankton.

Whale sharks are found in tropical and temperate waters. This largest of all fish can grow to 60 feet long. Scuba divers are delighted to swim alongside and sometimes hitch a ride on a whale shark.

Basking sharks grow to 30 feet long. They are named for their habit of lying at the ocean's surface, as if basking in the sun. With its mouth open—wide enough for a person to stand in—a basking shark swims through swarms of plankton, gulping down the tiny creatures.

In the 1970s, a Navy ship accidentally hauled in a shark never seen before. Scientists named it megamouth, which this 3-ton gentle shark certainly has!

Study the code box below, then see if you can label the shark parts and the three species of sharks.

1) 28–25–27–45–16 SHARK

2) 46–27–48–18–30–17–38 SHARK

	5	6	7	8	9	0
1	Y	E	N	K	R	C
2	H	P	A	W	M	T
3	D	O	J	G	V	I
4	L	B	Z	S	F	U

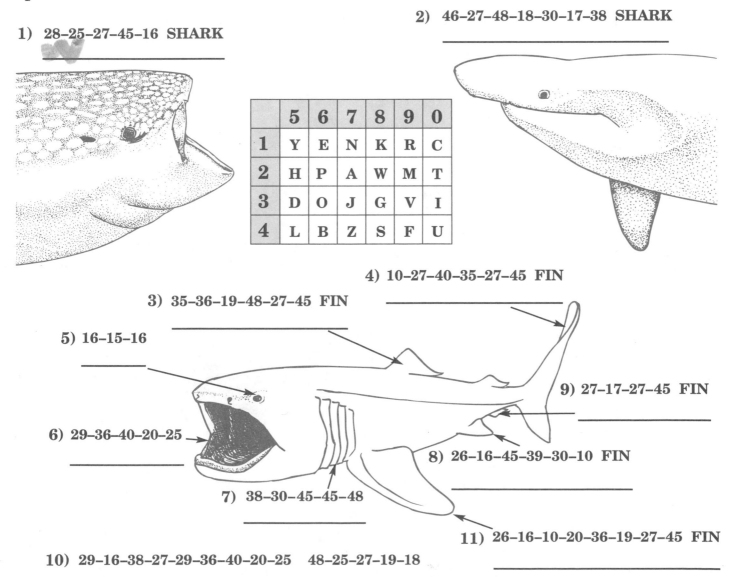

3) 35–36–19–48–27–45 FIN

4) 10–27–40–35–27–45 FIN

5) 16–15–16

6) 29–36–40–20–25

7) 38–30–45–45–48

8) 26–16–45–39–30–10 FIN

9) 27–17–27–45 FIN

11) 26–16–10–20–36–19–27–45 FIN

10) 29–16–38–27–29–36–40–20–25   48–25–27–19–18

THE HUNT IS ON!

All reptiles have a method of finding food. The rattlesnake has heat-sensitive pits in its face. It also has a scent-sensitive forked tongue to smell out its favorite food—rats.

While the rattler hunts its prey, the red-tailed hawk and king snake hunt the rattlesnake. The red-tailed hawk soars overhead and hunts with keen vision. A constrictor, the king snake can easily kill and eat a rattlesnake its own size.

Below, help the hungry rattlesnake find the rat. Be careful! The rattlesnake could become the prey.

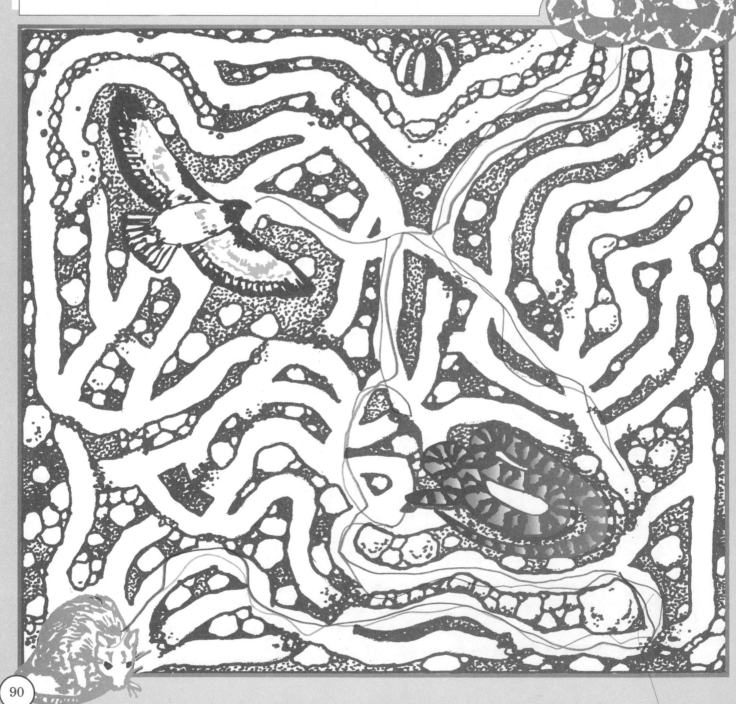

KING COBRA

Did you know that the king cobra is the largest venomous snake in the world? To find out more, fill in the missing vowels (a, e, i, o, u) below.

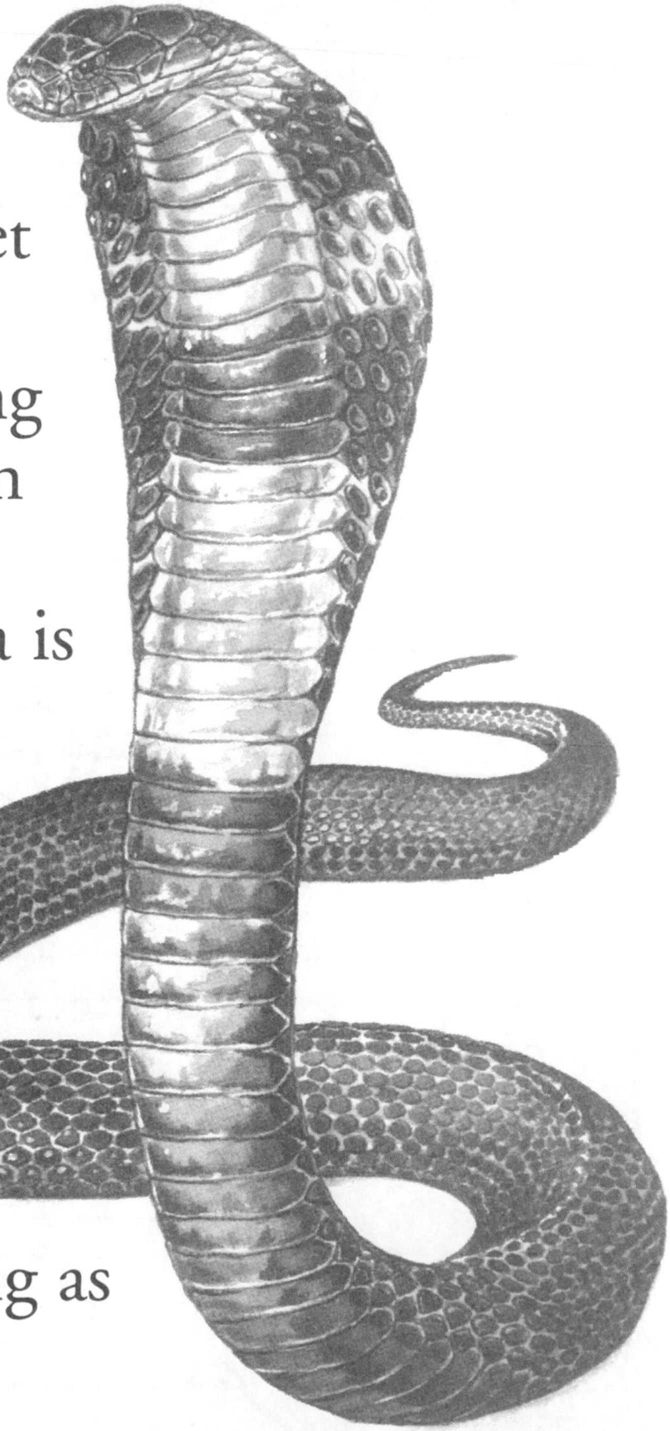

Northern Ind_a is home to the k_ng c_br_. An average ad_lt king cobra can gr_w to 15 f_ et long!

V_ry aggressive, the king cobra may attack a p_rs_n without even being pr_voked. The king cobra is the only sn_k_ to b_ild a n_st for its _ggs. The m_th_r gathers decaying leaves with the coils of her b_dy, and gu_rds the _ggs for as long as 80 days until they h_tch.

WEB WOLVES

Wolf spiders are some of the largest and quickest wandering spiders. They live in many different habitats, including people's houses. Although they are large and scary-looking, wolf spiders are not harmful. In fact, they are welcome in some homes, where they help control cockroaches, ants, and other household pests.

The wolf spider's name comes from the way the spider hunts and from its gray, hairy body. This large spider seldom weaves a web, but may dig a burrow where it will wait for an insect to walk by.

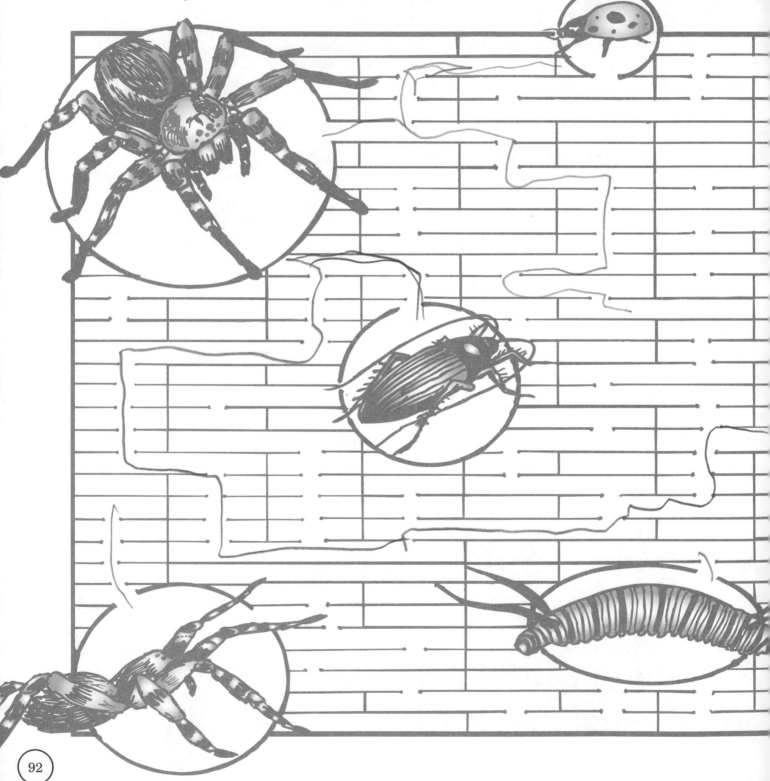

In the maze below, all five wolf spiders are all hungry. Which spider will get the prey? Only one—with your help!

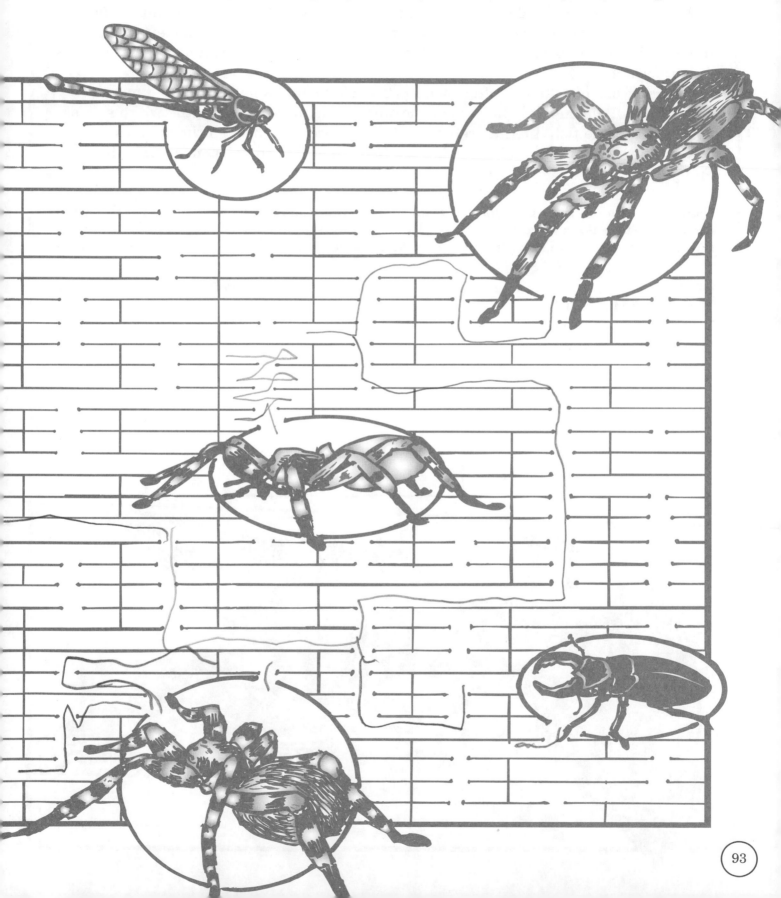

WHALE WORDS

Growing up to 80 feet long, the finback whale is the second-largest of all whales. Although it is called a finback, its dorsal fin is actually quite small. The finback is one of the few whales that has a different color on each side of its body. The left side of a finback's lower jaw is black, while the right side is white. This unusual coloration helps finbacks catch prey.

A group of finbacks will often swim in a circle to herd small fish into a massive ball. As small air bubbles churn near the surface, the finbacks flash the white side of their faces at the fish. Light is reflected off the white side through the bubbles, magnifying the whale's face and confusing the fish. Then the whale opens its mouth wide, and gulps!

Using the letters in the words *finback whales*, see if you can make at least 40 words. You can use a letter to make a word only as many times as that letter appears.
(For example, there are two *A*'s in *finback whales*, so no word can have more than two *A*'s.)

Score:

Three-letter words = 1 point

Four-letter words = 2 points

Five-letter words = 3 points

More than five letters = 5 points each

10-20 points: You're a minnow.

21-30 points: You're a shark.

31-40 points: You're an orca.

41+ points: You're a finback!

── Finback Whales ──

Where Bear?

Brown bears can be found in Europe, Asia, and North America. Perhaps the best-known brown bear is the mighty grizzly. This huge creature can grow to 10 feet tall and weigh more than 800 pounds. Male brown bears live alone, but females stay with their cubs for up to three years.

In cold climates, bears dig a den and make a bed of twigs and branches. After a summer of gorging on everything from salmon to berries, a bear enters its den and sleeps until spring. A layer of fat feeds the bear's body while it sleeps. In the spring, a very hungry bear awakens and is ready to start a new year.

Sometimes it is hard to tell one bear from another. Below are six pairs of brown bears. Look closely at the differences and see if you can match the pairs.

Mystery Penguin

Who goes there? All dressed up in formal wear, the only things this penguin is missing are the top hat and cane! Uncover this dapper dude by copying the shape in each numbered square on the left into the same-numbered box in the blank grid at right, and see who shows up! When your drawing is finished, unscramble the name below to find out what kind of penguin you have drawn.

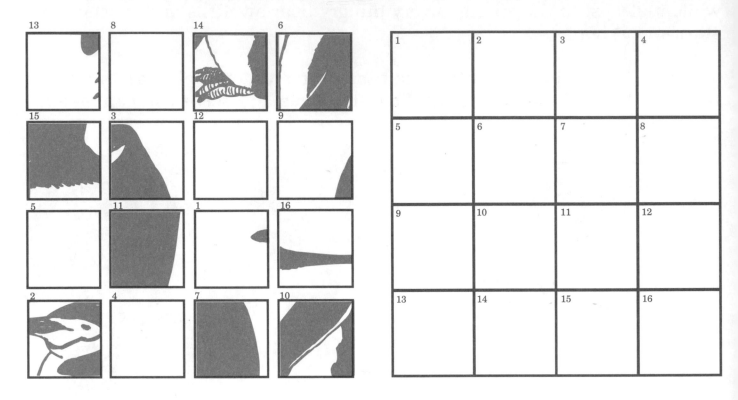

RANCTSHIP UGEINPN

_____ _____

ITSY-BITSY SPIDERS

Most female spiders make very good mothers. The nursery web spider builds a silk bed for her spiderlings and guards them until they are big enough to leave the nest and survive on their own. A crab spider guards her egg sac until she dies of starvation. One species of fishing spider carries her egg sac around with her wherever she goes. Her sac can grow so large that the mother is forced to walk on the tips of her feet. The wolf spider takes no chances—not only does she carry her babies on her back, but she attaches each baby to a safety line of silk in case it falls.

Most baby spiders do not closely resemble adults until they shed their carapace (outer skin), several times. In the puzzle below, match the spiderling siblings. There are six of each kind.

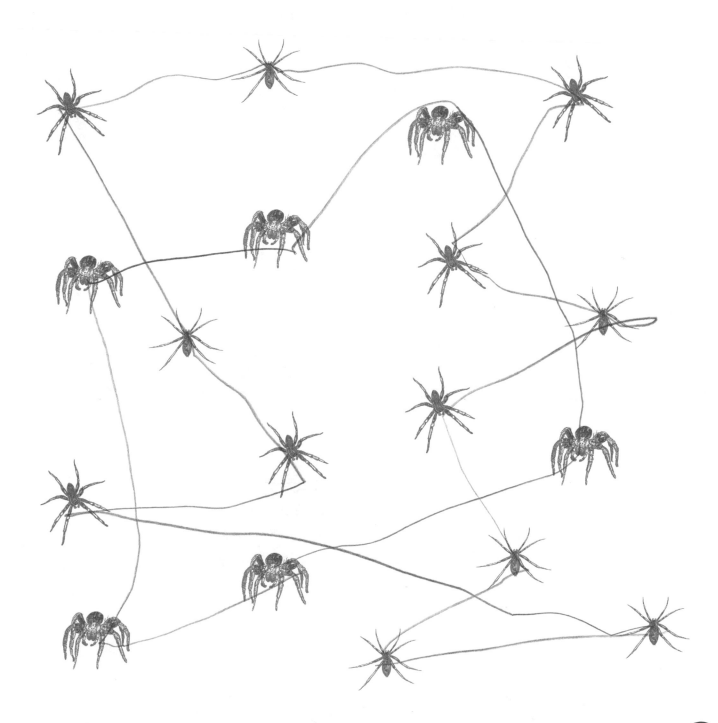

Bat Cave

Many bat species prefer to roost in caves. Sometimes millions of bats will live together in a colony. How many bats can you find in the cave shown here?

Big Brown and Little Brown

The little brown bat is one big helper when it comes to controlling mosquitoes. This three-and-a-half-inch microbat can eat about 150 mosquitoes in 15 minutes. There are 97 known species of little brown bats. They are the most common bats found in North America.

Big brown bats are some of the largest bats in North America—and they are only about 5 inches long! These microbats hunt close to the ground and fly slower than most bats.

Below is a small colony of big brown bats and little brown bats. Each one has a twin. Can you match up the pairs?

little brown

big brown

Predators

Sharks are among the world's best <u>predators,</u> which means that they hunt for <u>live</u> prey. Any vibration caused by a fish <u>attracts</u> a shark. <u>Movement</u> in the water is felt through a shark's <u>lateral</u> line. This is a line of nerves that goes from head to tail down the shark's sides and is connected to its nervous system. Sharks also have an excellent sense of <u>smell.</u> They can detect a small piece of tuna from 75 feet away.

With five rows of sharp <u>teeth</u>, sharks are well-equipped for the job of catching and eating prey. The fast-swimming <u>mako</u> shark has thin teeth for grasping and holding tuna—its equally quick prey. The white shark has <u>triangular</u>, saw-edged teeth that tear chunks out of sea lions and other large prey. The <u>tiger</u> shark has saw-edged teeth with curved tips that can grasp or tear just about <u>anything</u>.

When a shark bites, a flap of skin called the nictitating membrane *(NIK-tuh-tay-ting MEM-brayn)* covers and <u>protects</u> its eyes. This membrane is like an <u>eyelid</u>.

Based on what you have learned about sharks, complete the crossword below. If you need a little help, answers are underlined above.

Across
2. Fast shark
4. Five rows of _____
5. Shape of a white shark's teeth
7. Excellent sense of _____
9. Nictitating membrane ____ eyes
10. _____ prey
11. Attracted by _____
12. _____like flap over the eye

Down
1. Best _____
3. A moving fish ____ a shark.
4. Striped shark
6. Tiger sharks eat _____.
8. _____ line

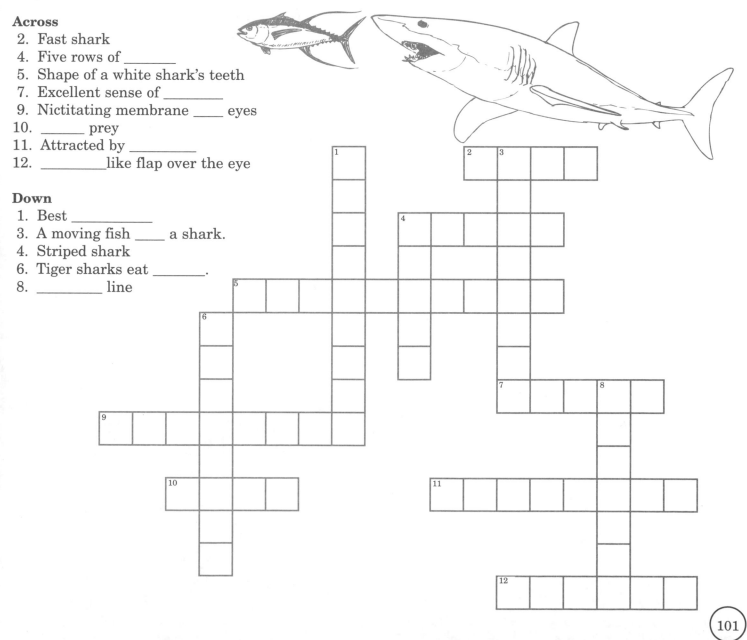

TRIASSIC TEASER

The first plant-eating dinosaurs appeared during the **Triassic** period (245 to 208 million years ago). Some of them belonged to a group called the **prosauropods** *(proh-SORE-uh-podz)*. The biggest and heaviest prosauropod ever discovered is the 40-foot-long *Melanosaurus (muh-LAN-oh-SORE-us)*, found in South Africa.

One of the smallest dinosaur skeletons (except for those still in **eggs**) found is the tiny skeleton of a baby *Mussaurus (muh-SORE-us)*. Its skull is just over an inch long and the entire **skeleton** fits into a man's cupped hands. *Mussaurus*, found in present-day

Argentina, was a prosauropod that lived about 215 million years ago. Its name means "**mouse** lizard."

Some of the earliest dinosaurs we know of—from as long as 225 million years ago—were meateaters. Lizard-hipped, meat-eating dinosaurs are called **theropods** *(THAIR-uh-podz)*. *Staurikosaurus (STAW-rih-kuh-SORE-us)* is one of the earliest dinosaurs known. This slim, seven-foot-long dinosaur ran on two legs. *Staurikosaurus* skeletons have been found in South America. Their sharp **teeth** and **claws** tell us that they ate meat.

Complete this puzzle using the bold-faced words above.
Two words have been started for you.

Name That Microbat!

Megabats may be bigger, but microbats rule when it comes to numbers. There are about 750 different microbat species! Discover the names of the five microbats shown here by working the rebuses below.

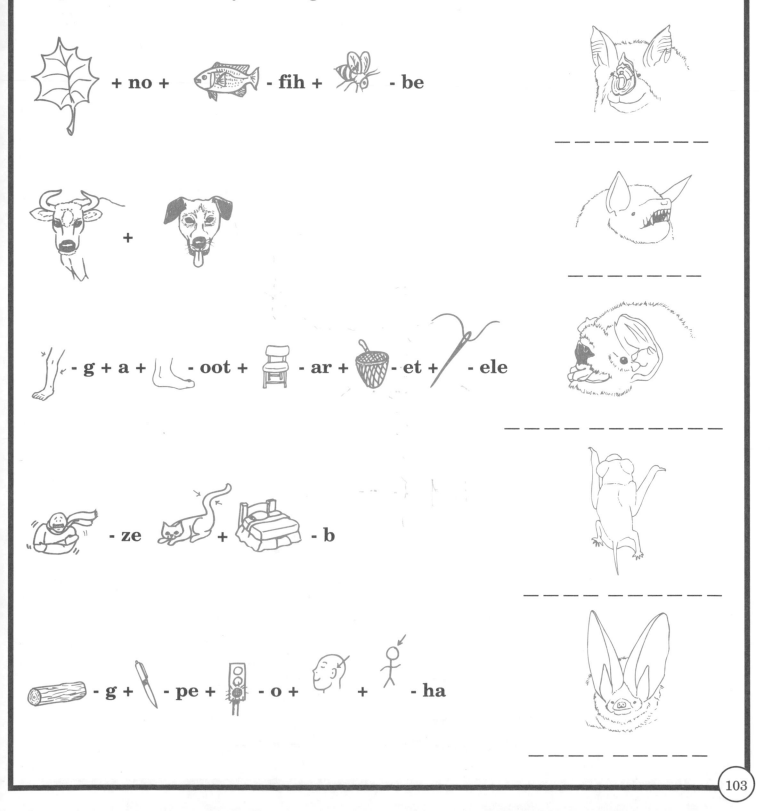

+ no + <fish> - fih + <bee> - be

_ _ _ _ _ _ _ _

<cow> + <dog>

_ _ _ _ _ _ _

<leg> - g + a + <foot> - oot + <chair> - ar + <basket> - et + <needle> - ele

_ _ _ _ _ _ _ _ _ _ _ _

<shiver> - ze + <cat> + <bed> - b

_ _ _ _ _ _ _ _

<log> - g + <pen> - pe + <traffic light> - o + <face> + <stick figure> - ha

_ _ _ _ _ _ _ _ _

Out of the Blue

The word search puzzle below is filled with words relating to whales. Use the list to help you find the words in the puzzle.

Baleen
Blowhole
Blubber
Bull
Calves
Cetacean
Dolphin
Dorsal
Fins
Fish
Flippers
Flukes
Lagoon
Mammal
Oceans
Porpoise
Predator
Shark
Toothed
Whales

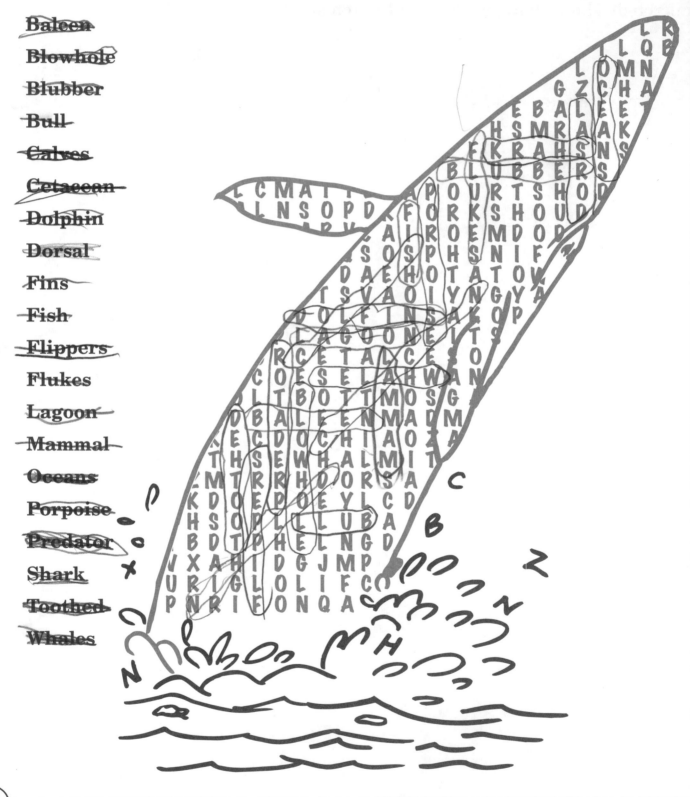

Look-Alikes

Imitation is a tool that spiders use to escape from predators or to catch prey. Often, a spider is mistaken for a branch or a piece of tree bark. The net-casting spider hangs motionless by its back legs, like a twig from a bush. It dangles above places where prey might pass. With its forelegs, the spider holds a net of silk that it quickly drops and wraps around its prey.

ant-mimic spider

Ant-mimic spiders have thin waists, and wave their front legs to look like an ant's antennae. Some species fool even the ants and are able to live among the ant colony.

Some insects look like spiders, but have very different characteristics. Spider beetles have antennae that look like spider legs. These beetles are not predators, like spiders, but are scavengers. They feed on animal droppings and decaying vegetation.

To work this crossword puzzle, unscramble the words below.

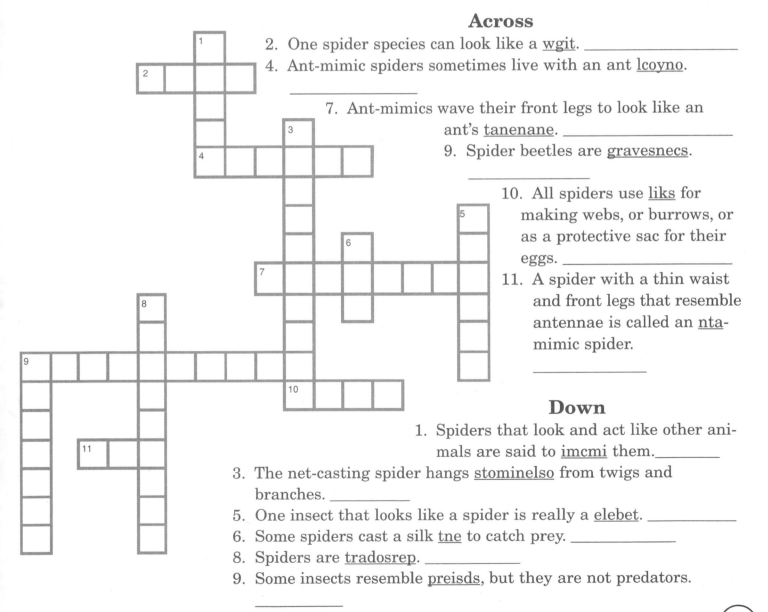

Across

2. One spider species can look like a <u>wgit</u>. _____
4. Ant-mimic spiders sometimes live with an ant <u>lcoyno</u>. _____
7. Ant-mimics wave their front legs to look like an ant's <u>tanenane</u>. _____
9. Spider beetles are <u>gravesnecs</u>. _____
10. All spiders use <u>liks</u> for making webs, or burrows, or as a protective sac for their eggs. _____
11. A spider with a thin waist and front legs that resemble antennae is called an <u>nta</u>-mimic spider. _____

Down

1. Spiders that look and act like other animals are said to <u>imcmi</u> them. _____
3. The net-casting spider hangs <u>stominelso</u> from twigs and branches. _____
5. One insect that looks like a spider is really a <u>elebet</u>. _____
6. Some spiders cast a silk <u>tne</u> to catch prey. _____
8. Spiders are <u>tradosrep</u>. _____
9. Some insects resemble <u>preisds</u>, but they are not predators. _____

Flying Reptiles

The first pterosaurs *(TER-uh-sores)*—flying reptiles—appeared in the Triassic period. The last ones vanished at the end of the Cretaceous period (145 to 65 million years ago). Pterosaurs are not dinosaurs, but they took to the skies during dinosaur times.

There were two kinds of pterosaurs. Those like *Rhamphorhynchus (RAM-fohr-ING-kus)* were quite small and had long tails. The other group, which included *Pterodactylus (TARE-uh-DAK-til-us)*, had longer necks and shorter tails than the first group.

Quetzalcoatlus (KET-sol-koh-AT-lus) was one of the biggest flying creatures of all time. It cruised over Late Cretaceous Texas on thin wings that may have stretched nearly 40 feet wide!

Three sets of flying reptiles are flying below. Can you match the pairs?

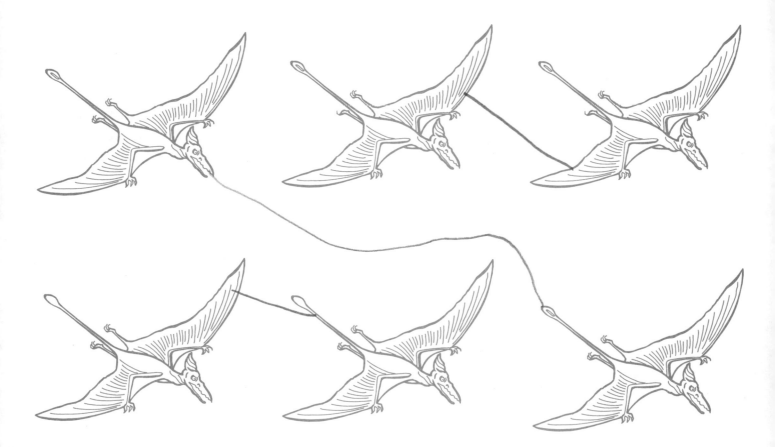

Mighty Mantas & Southern Stingrays

Rays are close cousins to sharks. They float along the sea bottom or fly out of the water using their huge pectoral fins, which can measure more than 20 feet from tip to tip. A Southern stingray has a sharp spike coated with slimy venom at the base of its tail, which it uses for protection. The giant, gentle manta ray is sometimes called "devil fish" because of the horns under its eyes, which help guide plankton into its wide-open mouth.

These two rays are hunting for a meal. Help the manta get to the plankton, and the stingray find a fish hiding in the sand.

manta ray

stingray

107

Creepy Crossword

While all spiders make silk, not all spiders weave webs. The trapdoor spider has a sneaky way of catching a meal. First it digs a burrow in the ground. Then it uses its silk to line the burrow. The trapdoor spider hides in the hole beneath a lid until it feels the tiny vibrations of prey walking by. Then the spider pops out and ambushes the prey.

The jumping spider uses strands of silk to secure itself to a leaf or twig while it launches itself at prey. The female also uses her silk to make a nest for her spiderlings.

Orb weavers spin webs and wait for prey to fly into the sticky traps. Most orb weavers will wrap up prey and save it for a time when food is scarce.

If prey gets tangled in a black widow's messy, disorganized web, the spider injects it with lethal venom. The black widow is one of the few spiders with a bite that can put a human in the hospital.

Test your knowledge of spiders.
Unscramble the words below, then use them to complete the crossword.

Across
4. Spiders hunt for <u>yrpe</u>.
5. Not all spiders weave <u>bswe</u>.
7. Spiders are classified as <u>hcsndiraa</u>.
8. Black widows weave <u>smyes</u> webs.

Down
1. Some spiders dig a <u>ubrwor</u>.
2. <u>vreey</u> spider has eight legs.
3. Some spiders use <u>ovenm</u> to catch their prey.
6. All spiders make <u>ksli</u>.
7. Trapdoor spiders <u>hmbasu</u> their prey.
9. <u>pjmngiu</u> spiders pounce on prey.
10. Spider webs are <u>cstyik</u>.

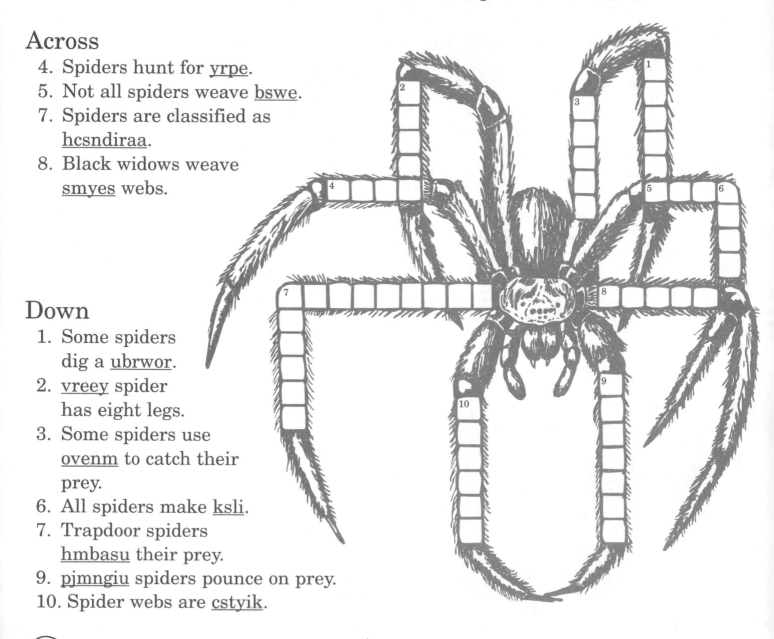

Tropical Teaser

Read the paragraph below. Then fit the bold words into the crossword grid and color the fish to complete your tropical habitat.

Coral reefs are home to thousands of species of **tropical** fish and other unique animals. Each animal has developed its own survival techniques, adapting to life in the coral reef. Brilliant **parrot** fish use their strong beaks to feed on hard corals. The **butterfly** fish uses its long snout to explore sponges for tasty treats, and it also has a false eyespot on its tail to fool predators into thinking that it is too big to eat. The **frog**fish disguises itself as a piece of red coral and waits for smaller fish to swim by. The batfish cruises the sand looking for prey. The **triggerfish** locks its dorsal fin around coral to hold itself in place where other animals can't reach it. **Moray** eels hide in caves, and **garden** eels burrow in the sand. Sea **horses** cling to soft corals and slurp up plankton as it floats by, and purple **sea fans** wave in the currents while beautiful angelfish look for food. Even the **corals** are animals. A coral reef is a colony of hundreds of thousands of tiny anemonelike animals living together.

TRICKY TARANTULAS!

One of the largest spiders in the world is the tarantula. About 30 species of tarantulas live in the southwestern United States. Although North American tarantulas are large, their bites are not dangerous. Their South American cousins, however, can deliver a deadly bite. The tropical bird-eating tarantula is as big as a dinner plate! It is the largest spider in the world. In South America, some people hunt and eat these large spiders.

To defend itself, a tarantula can rear up and show its fangs to try to scare off an attacker, or it may use its back legs to fling tiny, irritating hairs from its abdomen into the face of the attacker.

This picture is crawling with tarantulas. Can you find at least 10?

Big Beaks

Beaked whales have a look that really sets them apart. Ranging in size from about 15 feet to more than 40 feet, some look like giant bottlenose dolphins. A few species even have teeth that grow out and over the top of the beak.

Most beaked whales live, swim, and dive as a group. Like dolphins, beaked whales help one another. When one is injured, the group may hold it up at the surface so it can breathe.

About 19 different kinds of beaked whales have been identified, some with very strange names. In the rebus below, see if you can figure out the names of some of these whales.

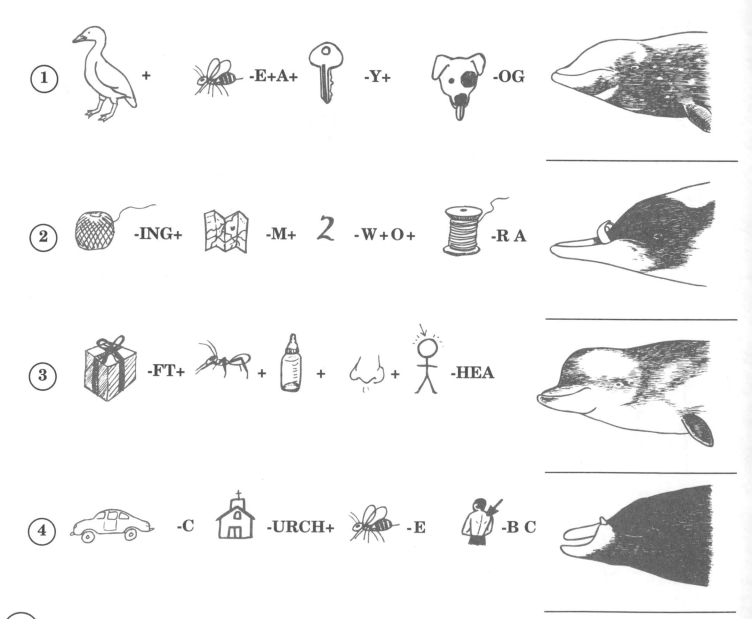

Bat Babies

Every spring, when bats wake from hibernating or return from their winter habitats, female bats have pups. The babies are born with strong legs and feet, and sharp claws. This allows them to cling onto their mothers or hang safely from the roost. Because they are small and hairless when first born, pups are gathered into a nursery with other baby bats for warmth.

Mother bats take turns baby-sitting the nursery so that each mother has a chance to go out and hunt for herself. When she returns, she locates her pup by the sound of its voice. It is not until after she smells and licks the pup that she is absolutely sure that it is hers. Only after it has passed these tests does she allow the hungry baby to begin nursing.

When it comes time to teach her pup how to fly, a mother bat takes her baby along with her on the hunt. Bat babies grow up quickly. They are flying and hunting on their own within one month of birth.

See if you can fill in the blanks below using your knowledge of bats. If you get stuck, decode the answer by using the code box.

Baby bats are called _____.

Baby bats are born _____.

It takes only about _____ _____ before a baby bat is flying and hunting on its own.

Mother bats form _____ to care for babies.

flying fox

Bat mothers take turns baby-sitting so that each one has a chance to _____ for food.

	I	⊤	⊥	‖	⊥⊥	⊤⊤
X	a	r	b	s	c	p
⊠	e	d	t	v	y	h
⋈	u	o	n	l	i	m

113

CAIMANS

The caiman is the South American cousin of the American alligator. Caimans liv[e] in swamps, rivers, and flooded plains. There are several kinds of caimans. The com[?] mon caiman reaches a length of only about eight feet. Can you name the type [of] caiman struggling with the anaconda in the picture below? As a hint, here is a riddl[e.] *This caiman may look like it is wearing glasses, but it does not have bad eyesight.*
Solve the rebus below to answer the riddle and name the caiman.

= <u>s p e c t a _ _ _)</u>

CAIMAN

THE BIGGEST SQUEEZE

Can you imagine a snake taking on an alligator? The anaconda can. Find out more below, and make the underlined words fit in the puzzle.

A N A C O N D A

The green anaconda is the heaviest snake in the world. It often preys on the caiman. The green anaconda is a constrictor, meaning that it squeezes its prey to kill it. The anaconda lives in rivers and swamps in South America.

Sharky Words

In addition to lots of sharp teeth, the shark below is hiding lots of sharky secrets. Use the word list to find shark names, behaviors, and body parts. The words go up, down, diagonally, backward, and forward. Words in parentheses do not appear in the puzzle grid.

Angel
Basking
~~Blue~~
Carpet
Cookie-cutter
~~Fish~~
Goblin
~~Great white~~

Hammerhead
Jaws
Mako
Pectoral (fins)
Predator
Reef
Silky
~~Six gills~~

Tail
~~Teeth~~
Thresher
Tiger
Whale (shark)
~~Whitetip~~
Wobbegong

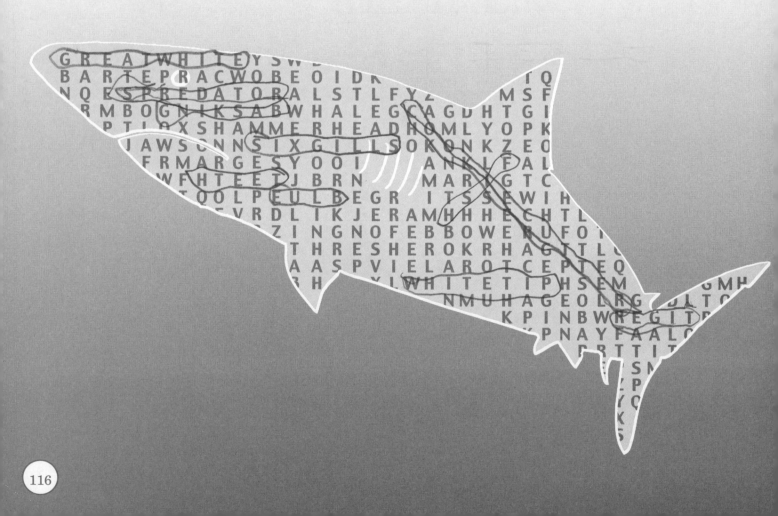

Ostrich Mimics

Read the paragraph below. Then fit the bold words into the crossword grid.

A group of ostrichlike **dinosaurs** lived during the late **Cretaceous** period (145 to 65 million years ago). They ran swiftly on long, thin hind legs. They probably ate small **reptiles**, mammals, and **insects.** Scientists think that they may also have eaten the **eggs** of other animals. The scientific name for this group of dinosaurs is ornithomimids *(OR-nith-oh-MYE-midz)*. It comes from two Greek words that perfectly describe what they are: *ornith*, meaning "**bird**," and *mimos*, meaning "imitator." Many ostrich mimics are known for their **speed**. Twelve-foot-long *Dromiceiomimus (DROH-mee-see-uh-MYE-mus)* may have been able to run up to 40 miles an hour! It could use that speed in two ways: to catch up to **prey**, and to escape from larger **predators**.

Endangered Bats

As is true of many other animal species, some bats are endangered. This means that certain species of bats may not survive unless they are protected from harm. There are too few in the wild to make enough babies to keep the species going.

Mexican long-nosed bats roost in caves in the southwestern United States and in

Mexico. They come out at night to feed on open cactus flowers, pollen, and cactus fruits. People like to visit the caves where the bats roost, which disturbs the bats. Although visiting a bat cave may be fun for people, this disturbance can kill thousands of bats. Mexican long-nosed bats are dying in areas where they once thrived.

The Mexican long-nosed bat in this maze is in search of a cactus flower. Help the bat get from the cave to the open flower and back to the cave. Be careful— the way out is not the same way in.

DEFENSE & DEFIANCE

Spiders are preyed upon by birds, lizards, frogs, and even other spiders. Spiders use a variety of methods to defend themselves or to escape attackers. Because venom is a valuable tool in catching prey, most spiders will use it as a last resort for defense, and only after warning an attacker. Instead, the spider may rear up to look larger and show its fangs, or it may simply try to run away.

Each species has its own defenses. Jumping spiders jump away from danger. Weavers may drop from their web on a silk lifeline into the bushes below. Wandering spiders are usually very quick and may run away from danger. Some forest spiders use camouflage to blend perfectly into the trees by looking like bark. Green lynx spiders live only on green plants, so they blend into their environment.

Using the code below, see if you can complete the following sentences about spider defenses. In the answers are circled letters. Unscramble the circled letters to spell out the bonus word. Each coded word is worth 10 points and the bonus word is worth 30. Check to see how you rate!

SCORING
90-120 points: You are a goliath tarantula.
60-80 points: You are a black widow.
40-50 points: You are a daddy longlegs! Don't get spooked—try again.
0-30 points: You are a spiderling. Read and try again!

	0	1	2	3	4	5
7	R	A	W	D	T	S
8	V	N	M	E	H	O
9	I	F	G	U	Y	P

1. Spiders would rather __ __ __ __ (○) __ __ than use their (○) __ __ __ __ for defense.
   07 39 18   17 27 17 49   08 38 18 58 28

2. Some spiders __ (○) __ __ out of sight when __ __ __ __ (○) __ __ __ (○) __ .
   37 07 58 59   47 48 07 38 17 47 38 18 38 37

3. Sometimes a threatened spider will make itself look larger by __ (○) __ __ __ __ __   __ __
   07 38 17 07 09 18 29   39 59

   and showing its __ __ __ __ (○).
   19 17 18 29 57

Bonus:
Unscramble the circled letters above to name a type of spider that will drop into the bushes on its silk if it is being preyed upon.

— — — — — — — —

Good Mother

The name *Maiasaurus (MY-uh-SORE-us)* means "good mother lizard." Paleontologist John Horner named this duckbilled dinosaur after he found fossils, in Montana in 1979, suggesting that it took care of its babies. Until *Maiasaurus* was found, scientists thought that dinosaurs just laid their eggs, then left the babies to take care of themselves after they hatched, as most reptiles do.

Three sets of *Maiasaura* have hatched. Can you match each baby with its identical twin?

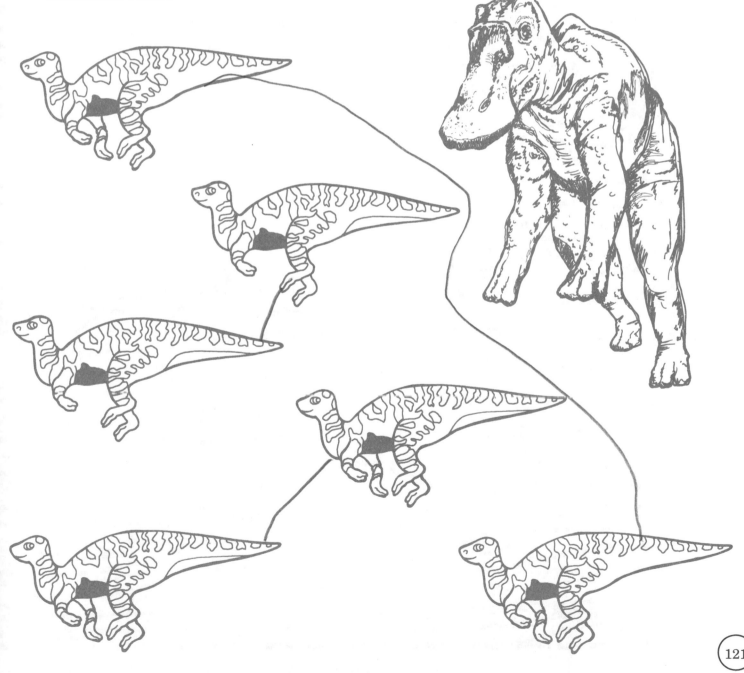

UNICORNS AND SEA CANARIES

Most people think of the Arctic as a harsh and icy place. But narwhals and beluga whales call this chilly habitat home.

Narwhals can grow to about 14 feet long, and the males have a special feature: The left front tooth grows through the upper lip into a tusk about 10 feet long. Some scientists think that the tusk is used to attract females, or perhaps to dig mollusks out of the sea floor. Whatever its purpose, the tusk makes a male narwhal look like a swimming unicorn.

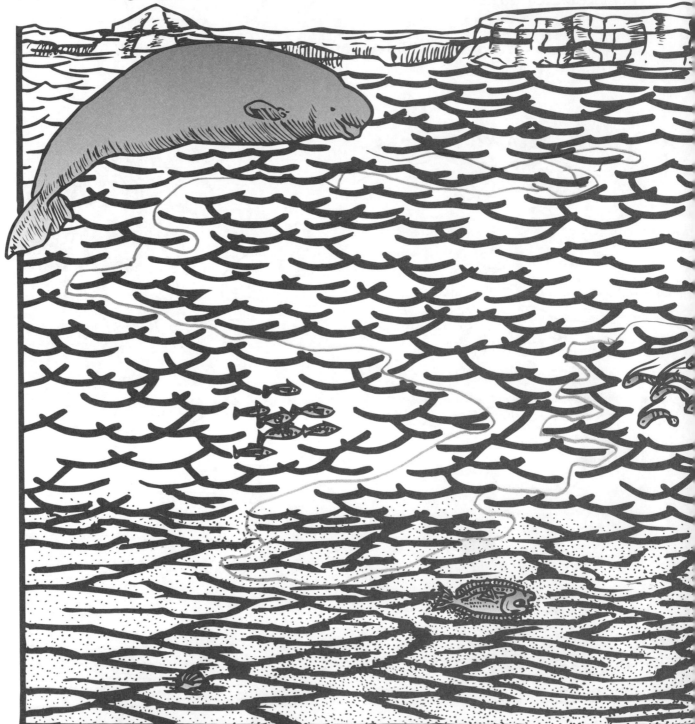

Like the Arctic ice that surrounds them, beluga whales are pure white. Belugas live in very large herds. Unlike other whales, the beluga can turn its head from side to side, which helps it spot enemies. Known as "sea canaries" because of their high-pitched chirping sounds, belugas may be able to "tell" each other when trouble is coming.

This narwhal and beluga are hunting. Help them get to their prey.
Each whale can get to only one type of prey.

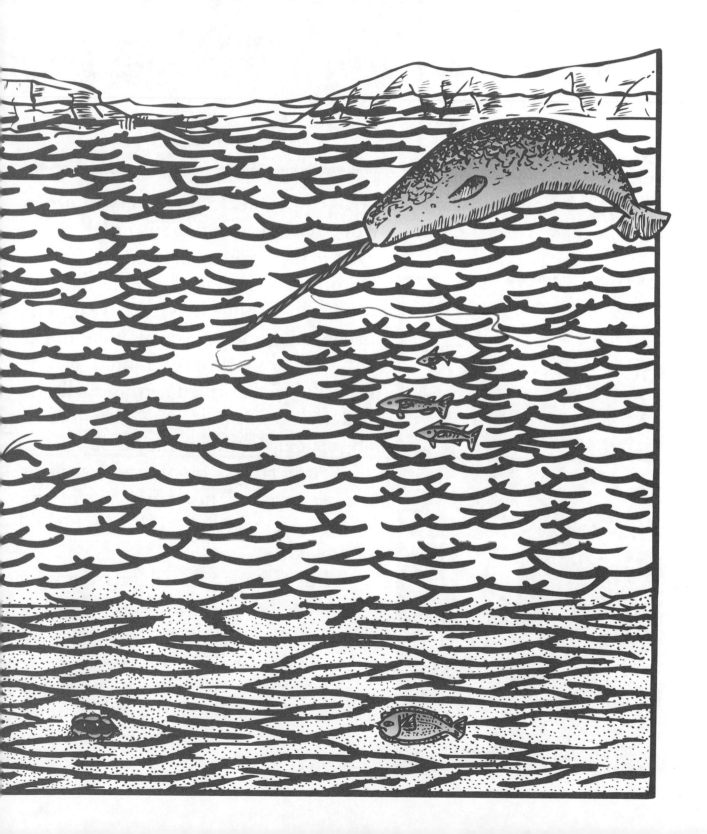

REPTILES OF THE SEA

The sea is home to many reptiles, including turtles.

Turtles are one type of marine reptiles. The largest is the leatherback, which weighs close to a ton.

Most marine turtles are endangered. The female turtles return each year to the beaches where they themselves were hatched, and lay their eggs there.

However, the eggs are often stolen by animals or people. Out of every hundred baby turtles that make it to the sea, only one will survive to adulthood.

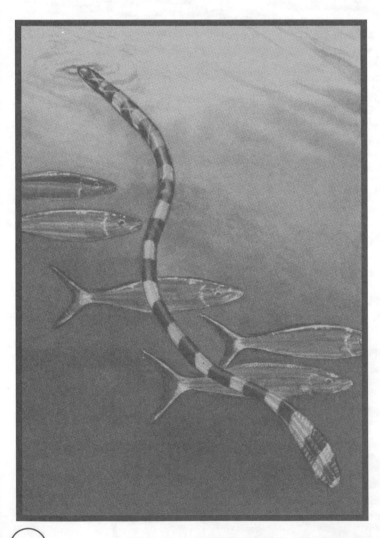

Turtles are endangered for other reasons as well. Many loggerhead turtles drown in fishing nets each year. The hawksbill, which has a beaklike upper jaw, has always been hunted for its beautiful shell. Called tortoiseshell, the material was used to make ornamental objects before the invention of plastic.

Another type of marine reptile is the sea snake. They have one of the most toxic venoms and will bite if provoked.

The Galápagos Islands in the Pacific are home to the marine iguana. This colorful reptile feeds underwater on marine algae growing on rocks.

The largest crocodile is the Indo-Pacific, or saltwater crocodile. This marine giant is the only crocodile that lives in the sea.

Can you unscramble the 12 underlined words, then make them all fit into the puzzle grid? One has been done for you.

esa esknas will usually not bite unless you provoke them.

_____ _____

The twearstal roclicode is the only reptile of its kind that lives in the sea.

_____ _____

A real creature of the sea, the rameni naugai searches for food on the sea floor.

_____ _____

The shlibwalk rutlet has a beaklike upper jaw. _____ _____

The abeltakcher treltu grows to be very big. _____

_____

Fishing nets are a real problem for the endangered egharlodge uterlt.

_____

_____

S
E
A

125

Shark Soup

More than 350 different types of sharks live in the oceans of the world. They range in size from the six-inch pygmy shark to the largest fish in the sea, the whale shark. Sharks are masters of their domain. They are built so well that in the last 150 million years they have hardly changed at all!

Most sharks hunt for food, but some species strain plankton from the water. Some live near the surface, while others live in the deep where there is no light.

Bottom-dwelling sharks feed on shellfish, such as clams and crabs, biting through the shells with specialized teeth. Although sharks are among the most feared of all animals, very few shark species ever attack humans.

There are more than 20 sharks in the picture below. See how many you can find.

The Tyrant

Tyrannosaurus rex (tuh-RAN-uh-SORE-us) may be the most famous dinosaur of all. At 40 to 50 feet long, this giant was one of the biggest meat-eaters to ever walk Earth. *Tyrannosaurus* teeth are one inch wide and up to six inches long. They are shaped to cut through flesh and bone. Scientists think that *Tyrannosaurus* could rip off a 500-pound chunk of meat with just one bite of its powerful jaws!

Tyrannosaurus rex belongs to a group of dinosaurs called tyrannosaurids *(tuh-RAN-uh-SAW-ridz)*. Tyrannosaurids were around for only about the last 15 million years of dinosaur time.

Using all the letters from the word *Tyrannosaurus*, see if you can make at least 40 words. Write them in the box below. Remember, you can use a letter to make a word only as many times as that letter appears. (For example, there are two *N*'s in *Tyrannosaurus*, so no word can have more than two *N*'s.)

Score:
Three-letter words = 1 point
Four-letter words = 2 points
Five-letter words = 3 points
More than five letters = 5 points each

10-20 points:	You are *dino bait*.
21-30 points:	You are a *T. rex-in-training*.
31-40 points:	You are a *dino wiz*.
41+ points:	You are *dino-mite!*

Tyrannosaurus

Spiders, Naturally

Spider behavior is as varied as the species themselves. In this word search puzzle, find the listed species and other spider-related words. Words may go up, down, backward, forward, sideways, or diagonally.

Words in parentheses do not appear in the puzzle.

```
A E T J U O I M B L G L G V B
N O I P R O C S I O W C U I L
U X F D I A F S V M B R Y B U
R V Y A G R E E N L Y N X R E
S Q M D W R N N G K U I L A B
E W A D S C N D N F B L Y T A
R J R Y E K T E M I P O K I R
Y X S L K S D V R I U I K O K
W D F O H L D R U B R V C N Y
E A S N O X V S B M S F I P U
B A G G R E S S I V E U T E S
X M N L Z E Y D C G C B P A I
E B I E H D K I N U T F C N J
X U V G K D F I H M I U C V B
R S A S H X T B H S F N L N L
V H E Q U N Y C H M C N V O H
I T W V U C B I W T R E S M C
W V N H R I N D J X Q L U I I
S C A F E G A L F U O M A C M
C S C D J F M R A O G V S E I
A C A R B D N E A Y I E T I M
I H U N T S M A N Q T U N C B
W H U Y C J S X T U S W A J P
I H D Y J R J M V K P X L A W
V E N O M O U S W O R R U B J
```

- Aggressive
- Ambush
- Blue bark (scorpion)
- Burrow
- Camouflage
- Daddy longlegs
- Fishing (spider)
- Funnel (web)
- Golden (silk)
- Green lynx (spider)
- Hunting
- Huntsman (spider)
- Jaws
- Mimic
- Mite
- Nursery web (spider)
- Purse (web)
- Sac
- Scorpion
- Tick
- Venomous
- Vibration
- Violin (spider)
- Weaving

WHO GETS THE FISH ?

The South American matamata (*MA-tuh-MA-tuh*) is an unusual-looking turtle. It has fringelike skin on its neck that moves in the water's currents like a worm and attracts prey. When fish come close to the wormlike movement, the matamata gulps them down.

The gharial (*ger-EE-ul*), a crocodile native to India, lives in freshwater rivers. It grows to 21 feet

long, but is not known to attack people. With a long, tooth-filled snout, the gharial snaps up fish.

In this maze, both the gharial and matamata want to eat. Which will get the fish?

Dozens of Dolphins

This picture shows a huge family of dolphins swimming in a pod. Among the dolphins are other cetaceans and sea creatures. How many dolphins can you pick out from this marine scene? There are at least 30. Color them as you find them.

Basic Bat Body

Bats have some basic physical features common to other mammals. They also have some specialized features that make them unique. A bat has eyes, ears, a nose, a mouth with sharp teeth, a tongue, two forelimbs and two legs, thin skin covered in fur, a tail, and claws on its thumb and toes. Although bats have legs, they cannot walk very well because their knees bend backward. However, their claws are strong and enable them to hang upside down from even the smallest crevice in the surface of rock.

A bat's wings are this mammal's unique feature. Made of two layers of skin stretched over light bones, the wings span from a bat's forelimbs down the sides of the body and partway down the legs. Each forelimb has four finger bones and a thumb that ends in a claw. Thumb claws and a claw on the second finger help a bat hold on to fruit while it hangs from a limb and eats.

Many bats have nose leaves. These folds of skin around the nostrils may help aim sound waves when a bat uses echolocation. Many bats also have large ears for capturing sounds when hunting.

brown bat

Based on what you have read above, can you unscramble the bat body parts below?

1. WSACL _ _ _ _ _
2. GNSIW _ _ _ _ _
3. GEFIRN OENBS _ _ _ _ _ _ _ _ _ _ _
4. BUMHT WALSC _ _ _ _ _ _ _ _ _ _
5. RFU _ _ _
6. SONE AESELV _ _ _ _ _ _ _ _ _
7. GERAL RESA _ _ _ _ _ _ _ _ _
8. HNIT KNIS _ _ _ _ _ _ _ _
9. SPARH EEHTT _ _ _ _ _ _ _ _ _ _
10. YEES _ _ _ _

long-tongued
fruit bat

134

Mystery Fisherman

The fishing spider spends its days floating on the leaves of water plants. Dipping its legs into the water, it picks up vibrations made by small fish or insects struggling on the surface. Like a real fisherman, it may use a "hook"—one leg dangled in the water—to capture a fresh meal.

To see the mystery picture, draw the image in each numbered box below in the same-numbered box in the grid at bottom.

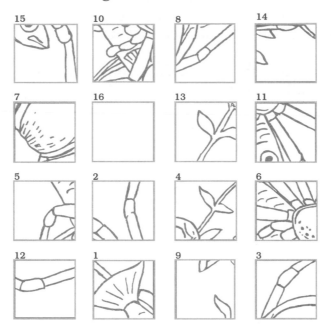

1	2	3	4
5	6	7	8
9	10	11	12
13	14	15	16

DOLPHINS

There are 32 different types of dolphins—more than any other animal in the cetacean family. Dolphins travel in groups called pods. They do this for protection and to catch food. Like most small whales, dolphins have teeth. Working as a team, dolphins circle around fish and herd them together. Then they take turns charging through the fish and eating them.

Each dolphin has its very own sound, which is made in its blowhole. To humans, the sound is like a high-pitched whistle. Dolphins also make clicking sounds, which help them find fish to eat. The clicks bounce off fish and come back to the dolphin. This echo makes a "sound picture" of the fish in the dolphin's brain, and is called echolocation.

Dolphins make other sounds to "talk" with each other. A mother dolphin will use her "voice" to call her baby.

In the maze below, help the Atlantic spotted dolphin through the maze of coral to get to a fish. It can get to only one fish!

Raptors—Birds of Prey

Raptors—such as eagles, hawks, falcons, and owls—hunt for food. They are birds of prey. An eagle, with its powerful wings and razor-sharp talons, can easily carry a large rabbit back to its nest. Some eagles are also scavengers. They will take food away from other birds or feed on carcasses, the dead bodies of animals.

Falcons, flying at a speed of about sixty miles per hour, are the fastest birds in the sky. Their hunting strategy is to dive on birds in flight and knock them unconscious with a stunning blow.

Turkey vultures have the best sense of smell of any living animal. While soaring high over their territory, they can easily detect a rotting carcass. All vultures are almost exclusively scavengers.

A nocturnal owl hunts with silent wings. Its hearing and vision rival other predators. An owl can't digest its prey's fur and bones, so they stay in part of the owl's stomach until it coughs up a "pellet." Researchers can tell exactly what an owl has fed on by examining the remains in the pellets.

All of the words underlined above are hidden in this word-search grid. Find them and circle them. They can be found going up, down, backward, forward, and diagonally.

```
Y O U C A N L U F R E W O P A L
G W T A L O N S P E L L E T S V
E Y E R P F O S D R I B S Y T U
T T S C H S I O B L H F I S I L
A U G A O U K H T O M P X L B T
R R W S E A N Y G S A I T W B U
T K N S A N Y T O N E E Y O A R
S E W E A G L E S H S T O T R E
M Y H S C A V E N G E R S I L S
E N F L I G H T N S T O M A C H
L K S Y R O T I R R E T U Y F O
L R I V A L W T N E L I S C A N
D I G E S T S L G M O E I T T I
D O O F A L C O N S R O T P A R
```

Finding Fruit

Not all bats use echolocation to find food. Some use their large eyes and good sense of smell to find their favorite foods, such as fruit, nectar, flowers, seeds, and pollen.

The bats in this maze include the flying fox, the tube-nosed bat, and the long-nosed bat. All are looking for a meal, but only one will find it.

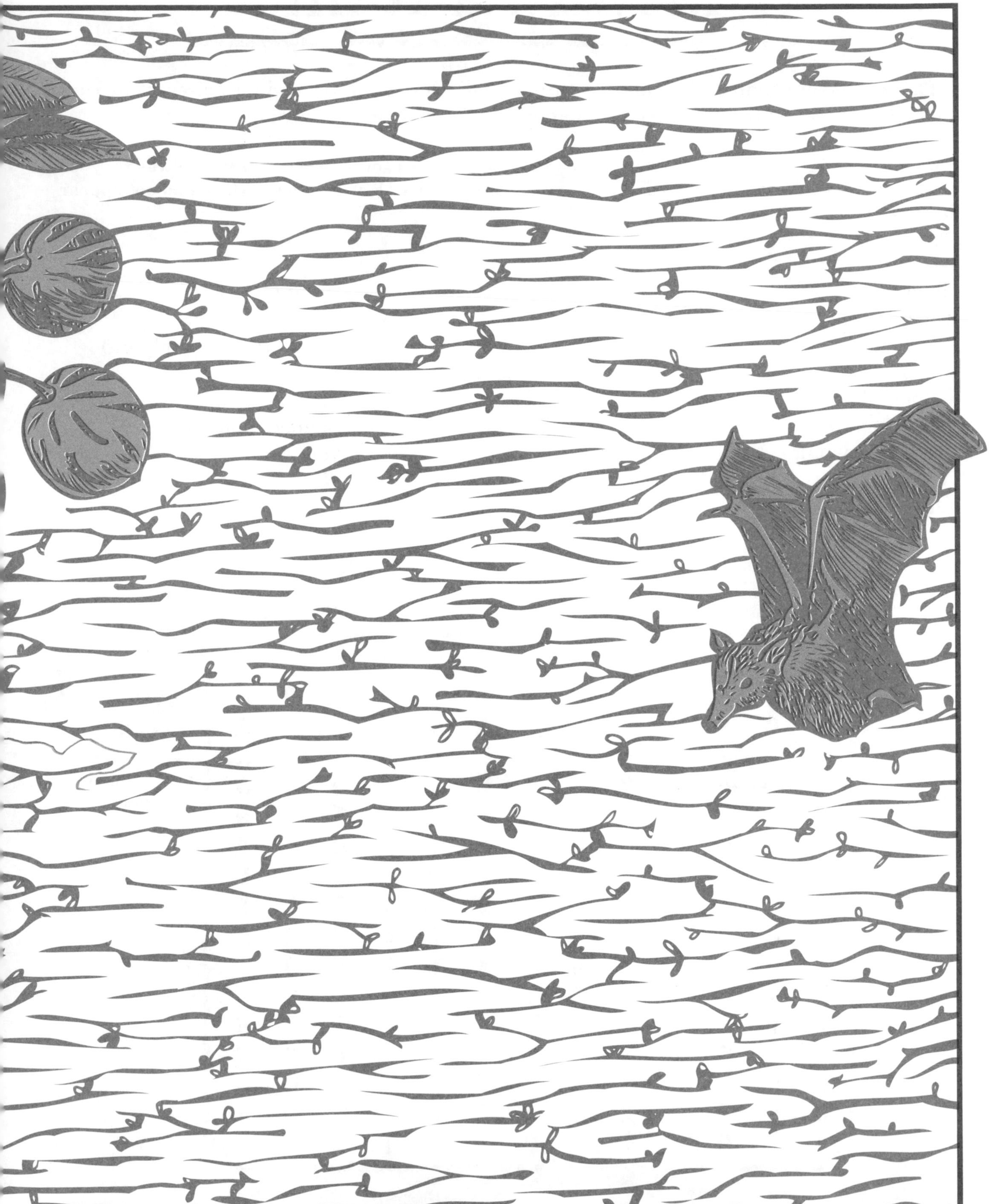

What's in a Name?

There are more than 70 species of cetaceans—whales, dolphins, and porpoises. They range in size from the little five-foot Hector's dolphin all the way up to the giant blue whale.

Find the words listed below in the puzzle grid. Many whales get their name from the way they look. What do you think the whale looks like when you hear the name? Words in parentheses do not appear in the puzzle.

Beluga
Black (dolphin)
Blue (whale)
Bottlenose (dolphin)
Common (dolphin)
Dusky (dolphin)
False killer (whale)
Finback (whale)
Finless (porpoise)

Gray (whale)
Harbor (porpoise)
Hourglass (dolphin)
Humpback (whale)
Minke (whale)
Narwhal
Orca
Pilot (whale)
Pygmy sperm (whale)

Right (whale)
Risso's (dolphin)
Rough-toothed (dolphin)
Sei (whale)
Spotted (dolphin)
Striped (dolphin)
Vaquita
White-beaked (dolphin)

hourglass
dolphin

pygmy sperm
whale

```
G O R I S S O S H A R D M
S H C O R G L A S B S P O N
R C O L U R K C A L N I F A
E O L T M O R R D U B P B R
L M U U P B I I E D F O O W
L M M M Y R G G I N H T T H
I O L Y G H T J R S K O T A
K N U S V T B O G C C Y L L
E S L P X L U R A L A P E S
S H E E L G E Z E B H V N A
L A B R I I N K A C B X O T
A Y A M G S S A E H I E S I
F U R B I B A C L G M E E U
O N O M S P S B E N K R D Q
H U M E P A T E K T I F W A
N D M K T T E D E P I O H V
S P O T T E D           R T S
```

hourglass dolphin

pygmy sperm whale

minke whale

Hidden Dinos

Two dinosaurs are hidden in the picture grid below. One is a plant-eater and the other is a meat-eater. Find out what they are by drawing the shapes in each numbered square on the left into the same-numbered space in the blank grid at right. Then, unscramble their names.

RNAUYNSRTAOUS XRE NDA IROTCAPRETS

_ _ _ _ _ _ _ _ _ _ _ _   _ _ _

_ _ _

_ _ _ _ _ _ _ _ _ _

HUNGRY HUNTERS

A spider has no ears. Instead, sensory hairs cover its entire body. Each hair is connected to nerves that are connected to the brain. When an insect walks by a spider, the hairs sense the movement and send a message along the nerves to the brain.

Spider hairs can also taste. Hollow hairs on the ends of a spider's legs and palps take in chemicals from food. So when spiders hold food with their legs and palps, they are probably tasting it.

In the maze below, all three spiders are hungry. The wandering spider (top left) is hunting for the grasshopper. The wolf spider (center left) is chasing the silverfish. The huntsman (bottom left) wants to catch the fly. Can you lead each one to its prey? Be careful! Coming face-to-face with another arachnid is deadly competition, and may be resolved only by a fight to the finish.

BOAS

Boas, which vary widely in color, are among the most beautiful snakes in the world. Patterns vary, even within a species. Below are five pairs of boa constrictors. Can you match each set of twins?

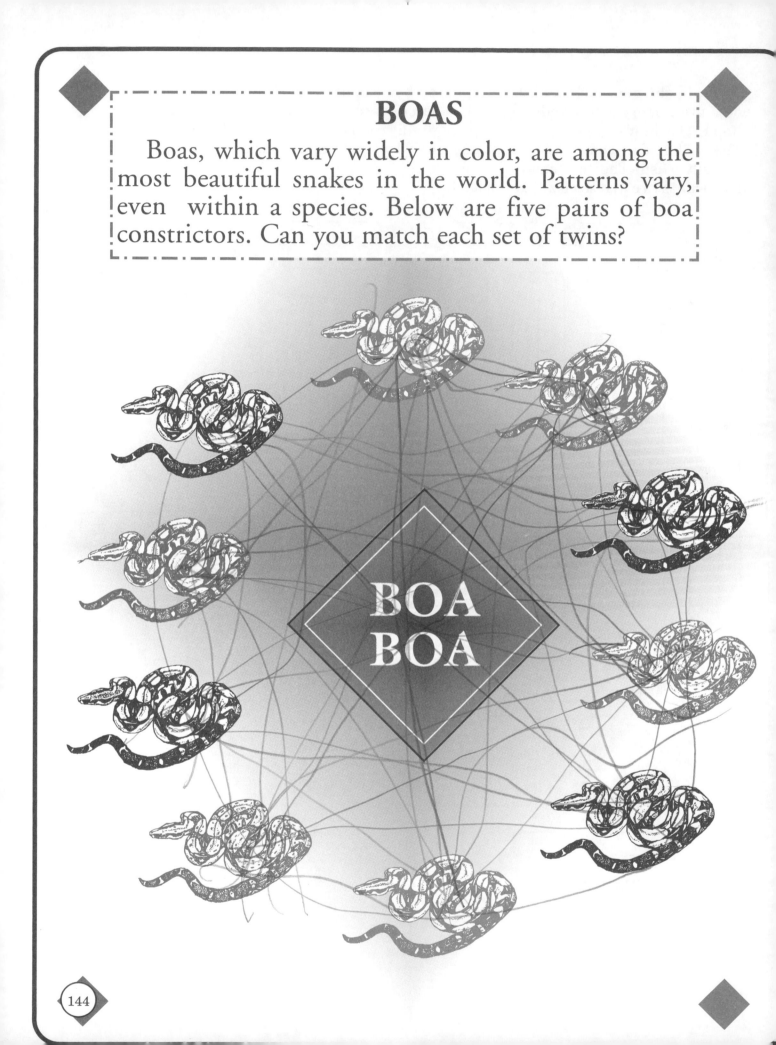

BOA
BOA

ALL ABOUT PYTHONS

The python family includes giant snakes and dwarf snakes. The reticulated python—the longest snake in the world—may grow to over 32 feet long. Pythons are found in Africa, Asia, and Australia. They prey on a variety of animals, including rodents.

Pythons are cold-blooded, or ectothermic *(ek-tuh-THUR-mik)*, which means that they rely on their environment to keep them warm. Unlike their boa cousins, pythons lay eggs. The mother may keep the eggs warm until they hatch by coiling around them and contracting her muscles. This raises her body temperature and warms the eggs.

Some people think that pythons make great pets. Burmese, ball, rock, and blood pythons are some of the species kept as pets.

To work this crossword, unscramble the words below.

ACROSS:

1. Pythons lay _____. (sgeg)
2. Another word for huge._____ (taing)
4. Another word for biggest. _____ (glestar)
6. This python is called by this name, but it's not hard as a _____. (korc)
8. Largest python. _____ (dreatilecut)
9. A word that means "very small." _____ (frawd)
10. Continent connected to Europe. _____(isaa)
12. An Asian country. _____ (niadi)
14. Python from Burma. _____ (mebruse)

DOWN:

1. Another word for cold-blooded. _____ (chotetcrime)
3. Rainforest python. _____ _____ (engre erte)
5. Round python. _____ (lalb)
7. The name of the red liquid that runs in an animal's veins is also the name for this python. _____ (dolob)
8. Pythons prey on _____. (storden)
11. A continent. _____ (raltuasia)
13. People keep pythons as _____. (step)

Jewels of the Reef

Thousands of species of brilliantly colored fish call the world's coral reefs home. Some of these fish are tiny enough to hide in the pores of sponges, while others weigh hundreds of pounds each.

More than 70 tropical fish are swimming in this coral-reef scene. How many can you can find? Coloring them as you go is the best way to find them all.

Feline Frenzy

serval

The largest cats—lions, tigers, jaguars, leopards, and cougars—roar! The cheetah is in a class by itself. Unlike other big cats, cheetahs neither roar nor retract their claws. Smaller wild cats, such as the ocelot, fishing cat, and Geoffrey's cat, as well as domesticated cats, make a variety of purring and mewing sounds.

Most people are more familiar with the names of big cats than with the many domestic cat names, such as the hairless sphynx and the tailless manx.

In the word search below are cat names, behaviors, and traits going up, down, backward, forward, and diagonally. Words in parentheses are not in the puzzle.

leopard cat

```
J R T O S L A B Y S S I N I A N S W
A A A O E D M A R X N Y L D D O I O
G G B N R M A I N E C O O N P R A D
U U B L V T D R H R A D D U C E M F
A O Y F A O O R A N E S R R A G E I
R C E C L G T I R O I R E A R I S S
W K B X N Y H P S V R S A U A T E H
N O D N I I N A T E H I W G C O S I
B R E A S H F N B D S O R A A L O N
E A S M M S T T S L H H E J L E C G
H T A D S I O H M E U D E C O C I A
S Y E R F F O E G G S E E L A O L H
I E I O W P E R S I A N O I L T A S
I N A Y A L A M I H A T E E H C C J
```

Abyssinian
bobcat
calico
caracal
cat
cheetah
cougar
fishing (cat)
Himalayan
jaguar
jaguarundi
korat
lion
lynx
Maine coon
manx
meow
ocelot
panther
purr

roar
serval
Siamese
sphynx
tabby
tiger
tortoiseshell

bobcat

Designing Dolphins

Dolphins are shaped like torpedoes. They are perfectly designed for cutting through the water and swimming at more than 30 miles per hour! With its powerful flukes, a dolphin can launch its heavy body up to 22 feet in the air to perform amazing acrobatics.

Most dolphins have the same basic shape with slight variations. Follow these simple steps to learn how to draw a dolphin. Use a pencil so that you can erase guidelines as you go.

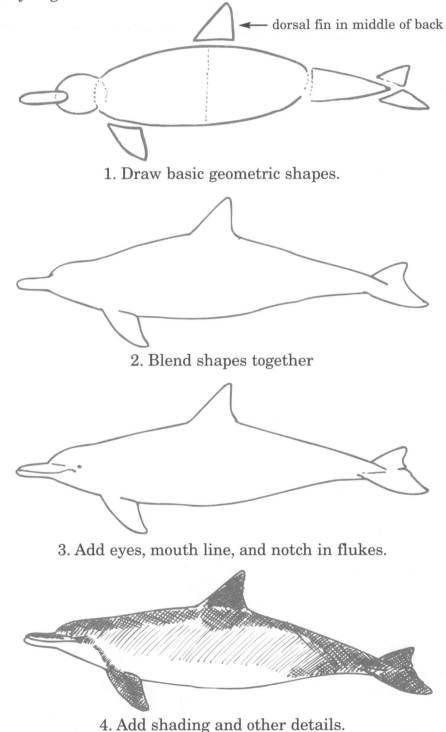

← dorsal fin in middle of back

1. Draw basic geometric shapes.

2. Blend shapes together

3. Add eyes, mouth line, and notch in flukes.

4. Add shading and other details.

Gone Batty!

In the picture below, you will see many types of bats roosting and flying around. How many can you find? There are at least 20 bats in this picture. A helpful hint: Color each bat as you find it.

SMILE!

A smiling face is hiding in the grid below! Put the pieces together by drawing what appears in each numbered square on the left into its correct space in the grid. Then see if you can identify this species, known for its smile. Hint: Unscramble the name when you have finished your drawing.

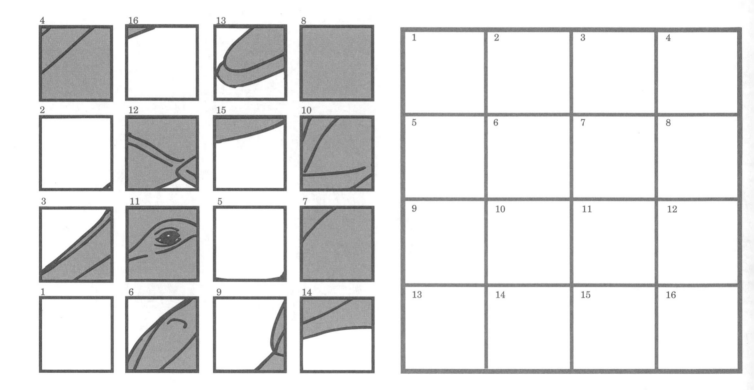

TOOTSLBEEN   PNIDHOL

_ _ _ _ _ _ _ _   _ _ _ _ _ _

Finding Bats

In this word search puzzle, you will find the names of 24 types of bats. As you can see, the names are very descriptive. They give you an idea what each bat looks like. Names may be found going up, down, forward, backward, and diagonally.

naked bat

wattled bat

wrinkle-faced bat

```
T D X S J P M O S S O L B I W R D B S
Z E L W O U O Y B A L F I N G E T A S
O C T O D R M L U N I L S N O S K T E
A F R R K R N M T I D L S N L E W L N
L W I D E L A F T E E A F T D W I I W
I O P N M E M S R E L L T W C N N K R
T L L O L A A N E F A A W N A O G S I
T L E S T M A G R L A P R B F R E D N
E O N D O C O G L I P E P N F B D E K
G H O J S C O B Y V E P N S E W P R L
O A S G I N O L S V T S M A W G B O E
B R E M N L C B E E A W B A P R O L F
L Y L R O A K E Y W R O A I R E L C A
I M E M C T O L S O E L F S C J S I C
N M A O H E I C L T D F C T A M C T E
A R F R T I B E S O G W A R M I M R D
R O U T E A S D B I T I L K E D A A O
T W L I A S T S A G W E N G E D A P R
O W L E S T S A G W I N G E D A P B
```

American leaf-nosed

Bent wing

Blossom

Brown flower

Butterfly

Chocolate

Dawn

Evening

False vampire

Flower-faced

Ghost

Hoary

Hollow-faced

Lalappet-eared

Least sag-winged

Little big-eared

Little goblin

Naked

Slit-faced

Sword-nosed

Tomb

Triple nose leaf

Wattled

Wrinkle-faced

153

SPIDER SAFARI

Can you find at least 35
spiders hidden in this picture?
Circle each as you find it. Look
carefully. Certain spiders are hiding
and can be tricky!

Where's Baby?

Penguins help each other baby-sit. Parents take turns hunting for fish while babies wait in a crèche, or nursery, far inland. Sometimes it is hard for a returning parent to find its baby among the thousands of penguin chicks all crying for a meal. But each parent knows its own baby by its unique call.

Help this penguin mother find her way through the crèche to her hungry baby.

Here, Kitty Kitty!

A big cat's coat helps it blend into its environment. In the puzzle below, one large cat is well-camouflaged, but you can help bring it into the open. Draw the shapes and lines from each square in the same-numbered square in the empty grid.

Can you identify the hiding cat? Here is a hint: It is the largest member of the cat family. If you need more help, unscramble the name below the grid.

BRAINISE GRITE _____

PALAEOSCINCUS
How to Draw

Plant-eating armored dinosaurs lived during the Cretaceous period. They relied on their armor to keep them from becoming another dinosaur's lunch. Armored dinosaurs belong to a family called Ankylosauria *(an-KYE-loh-SORE-ee-ah)*. That name means "fused lizards."

Palaeoscincus (PAY-lee-oh-SKINK-us) means "ancient skink," because the animal's teeth resemble those of a modern skink (a type of lizard). *Palaeoscincus* was discovered when scientists found one tooth in Montana.

Draw a *Palaeoscincus* by following the four steps below. When you are finished, color your *Palaeoscincus* and draw in a prehistoric setting. Have fun!

1. Begin by drawing a large oval for the body and two circles for the head. Attach the tail, adding two egg-shaped ovals at the tip.

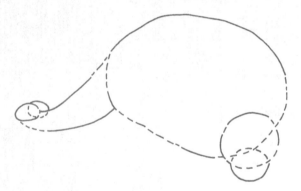

2. Add the legs and claws. Next, carefully add rows of triangular spikes all over the body, head, and tail.

3. Complete the face, then blend all the separate shapes into a smooth outline of the dinosaur's body. Be sure to erase any lines you no longer need.

4. Now use your imagination to fill in the details. What color or colors do you think this dinosaur was? No one really knows, so use your favorite colors to complete *Palaeoscincus*.

WORD WEB

Wandering spiders make up a large family. Using the letters in the words *wandering spiders,* see if you can make at least 25 other words. Remember, you can use a letter only as many times as it appears. (For example, there are 2 *S*'s and 2 *E*'s but only one *W*.) Make sure that each word has at least three letters in it. Give yourself 5 points for each three-letter word, 7 points for each four-letter word, 10 points for each five-letter word, and 15 points for each six-letter word. Then add up your score!

Bonus: Give yourself an additional point for every word you think of after the first 25 words. There are lots of words to create! Have fun!

Wandering Spiders

Thar They Blow!

Can you find all the whales, dolphins, and porpoises in this picture? There are more than 30.

Dolphin Match-Up

Some species of dolphins look very much alike. A few related species live in different oceans or hemispheres.

The Pacific whitesided dolphin and its look-alike cousins, the dusky dolphin, live in different hemispheres of the Pacific Ocean. The Pacific whitesided lives in the Northern Hemisphere, and the dusky in the Southern. Over in the Atlantic Ocean, thousands of miles away, lives another close cousin—the Atlantic whitesided dolphin. Although it is a little larger than its Pacific Ocean cousins, all are very similar.

Look carefully at the differences among these dolphins. How are they alike? How are they different? See if you can match up the families. There are three Atlantic whitesided dolphins, four dusky dolphins, and five Pacific whitesided dolphins.

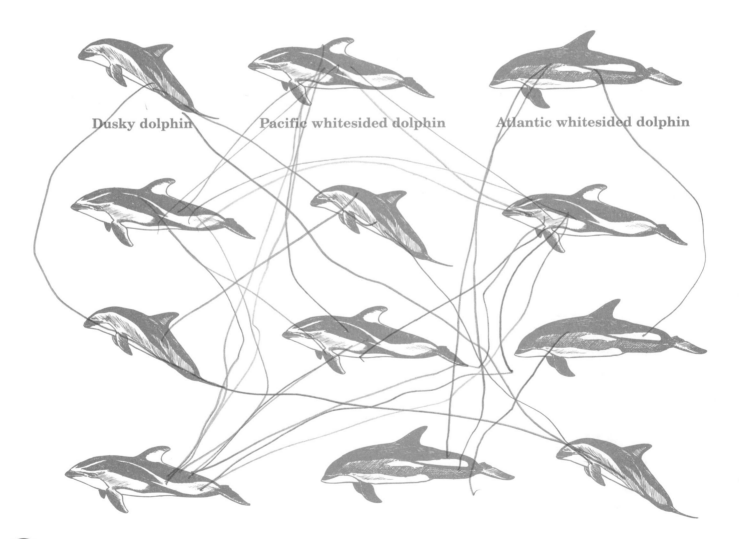

Dusky dolphin   Pacific whitesided dolphin   Atlantic whitesided dolphin

Hearing Their Way

Have you ever heard the saying "blind as a bat"? As you have already learned, bats aren't blind at all. Microbats have small eyes, and can see in daylight. However, these bats hunt mainly at night, which means that their eyesight isn't very useful. Instead, microbats echolocate.

A microbat can hear so well, it can tell the difference between a mosquito and a gnat! Some microbats have ears as large as their entire bodies. Big ears help the bats trap more sounds—a useful feature, because microbats hunt insects, small fish, frogs, and birds.

Bats echolocate differently. Bats with "nose leaves," such as the horseshoe bat, produce echolocation sounds (ultrasound) through their noses! Many experts believe that they also use their "nose leaves" to control the direction the sounds will go.

In the maze below, a horseshoe bat is chasing its dinner. Which insect will it catch? Help the bat find its meal.

Triceratops Lost

In the maze below, a young *Triceratops (try-SER-uh-tops)* has been separated from its mother. Help this young dinosaur find its way back to safety, but beware! Many hungry predators would like to eat this little dino for lunch.

Vampire

People have long feared and misunderstood bats. No bat has a worse reputation than the vampire bat, the only bat that feeds on blood. The fact is that vampires rarely bite people or kill their prey. Found in Mexico, Central America, and South America, these bats feed on the blood of cattle, horses, and other livestock. The bat cuts a shallow wound and licks the drops of blood, sometimes just one ounce a night.

See how many words you can make out of the words *vampire bats*. Be sure that each word has three or more letters and use each letter only once per word. Give yourself 1 point for each three-letter word, 2 points for each four-letter word, 3 points for each five-letter word, and 5 points for each word with more than five letters. Add up your points and check the chart below to see how well you did.

10 - 20 points: You are a baby bat.

21 - 30 points: You are a little goblin.

31 - 40 points: You are a big brown bat.

41+ points: You are Count Dracula!

How to Draw the Lionfish

Fish have developed many defenses to protect themselves from predators. Most hide by blending into their surroundings. Others have bright colors and flashy fins, like the lionfish. Predators avoid the lionfish because they know that it carries a powerful punch—poison—in the rays of its fins. One taste of that poison teaches predators that this beautiful fish is not to be messed with.

Draw a lionfish using the four steps below.

1. With a pencil, lightly sketch a triangle for the face and free-form shapes for the body and fins. These guidelines can be erased as you complete your drawing.

2. Draw the eyes, mouth, gills, and the back. Notice the fringe shapes at the corners of the mouth. To begin the fins, sketch and erase to draw only the rays, as shown.

3. Add the fleshy membranes between the rays, then trace the intricate detail outlines. The details vary from fish to fish, so don't worry if yours is a little different.

4. The final details look more complicated than they are—just take it shape by shape. Some solid stripes and some lighter, broken-shaded stripes will add realism to your final lionfish drawing.

POISONOUS LIZARDS

The Gila *(HEE-luh)* monster and the beaded lizard are the only two poisonous lizard species in the world. Both are native to the dry deserts of the southwestern United States and Mexico.

These beautiful lizards were built for the harsh environment of the desert. Both have long claws for digging, thick beadlike scales to protect their skin and conserve water, and a fat tail. The fat in the tail is a source of energy to the lizards when prey is scarce.

The slow-moving Gila monster and beaded lizard hunt a variety of prey, including rodents, baby animals, other lizards, eggs, and other things that can't run away. They don't have fangs—they must chew their poison into prey. Their striking yellow-and-black or red-and-black coloration warns predators to stay away!

Using the code below, see if you can complete the sentences about the Gila monster and beaded lizard. Within the answers are circled letters. Write down all the circled letters, then unscramble the bonus word. Each coded word is worth 10 points. The bonus word is worth 30.

70-100 points: You are a Master Komodo!
50-70 points: You are a Gila Kid.
40-50 points: You are a Lizard Watcher.
Below 40 points: You are Lizard Prey.

1) The one thing that sets the Gila monster and beaded lizard apart from other lizards is:

__ __ __ ◯ __ __.
C5 A2 C3 B1 A2 A5

2) The Gila is __ __ __ __ and __ __ ◯ __ __
     B1 C1 A2 B3   C5 A3 B2 C4 B1
on animals that can't __ __ __ __ __ __ __.
     A3 B5 A5 A1 B3 A1 C4.

3) The beaded lizard's __ __ __ __ ◯ __ ◯ __ __ __
     A4 A2 C1 A2 A3 A1 C2 C3 A2 A5
warns __ __ ◯◯ __ __ __ __ __ to stay away.
   C5 A3 B2 B4 A1 C2 A2 A3 B1

	1	2	3	4	5
A	a	o	r	c	n
B	s	e	w	d	u
C	l	t	i	y	p

BONUS:
The Gila monster and beaded lizard survive in a
__ __ __ __ __ __ environment.

168

Snakes of Venom

Find your favorite venomous snakes in this word search puzzle. You also can find a few other things that have to do with snakes. The words can be found going up, down, forward, backward, or diagonally.

Banded krait
Bite
Bushmaster
Camouflage
Copperhead
Coral snake
Cottonmouth
Eyelash viper
Fang
Forked tongue
Gaboon viper
Hiss
King cobra
Palm viper
Paralyze
Pit viper
Prey
Puff adder
Rattlesnake
Rodents
Scales
Sea Snake
Shed
Sidewinder
Spitting cobra
Taipan
Venom

```
R E Y E L A S H V I P E R N T R
O L R N A C O T T O N M O U T H
D N S P B O E L K R G S L M Z B
E N B A N D E D K R A I T P M W
N U S L S F C I H V K A R O M M
T C U M P G H E S S I H G O S N
S A T V I Z C K T P K L N F T C
X M R I T M K A A R S E Z O Z K
Y O W P T L E N U F V P X R E W
K U R E I I K S R V U E W K K Y
I F E R N H A E E W Z Z B E A R
N L D S G G N L P M X Y U D N U
G A N H C R S T I A B L S T S Q
C G I E O Y A T V G E A H O L N
O E W D B K E A T N T R M N A M
B S E U R C S R I A I A A G R H
R E D D A F F U P F B P S U O G
A Q I U S C A L E S Y R T E C C
E R S T U C O P P E R H E A D E
Z P G A B O O N V I P E R T F A
```

Answers

Page 7

1. animals, adapted
2. plankton
3. food chain
4. jaws
5. oxygen, gills
6. wings
7. blubber, cold
8. oceans

Bonus Question: microscopic

Page 12

lizards
tortoises
crocodiles
snakes
turtles   Mystery Word: scales

Page 8-9

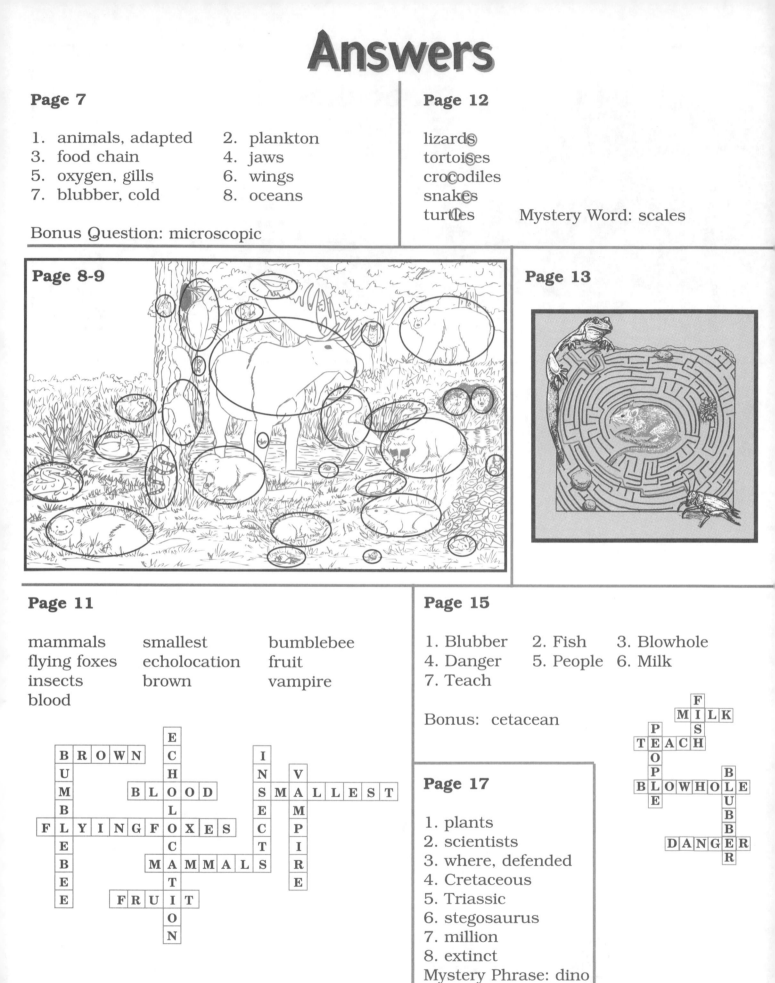

Page 13

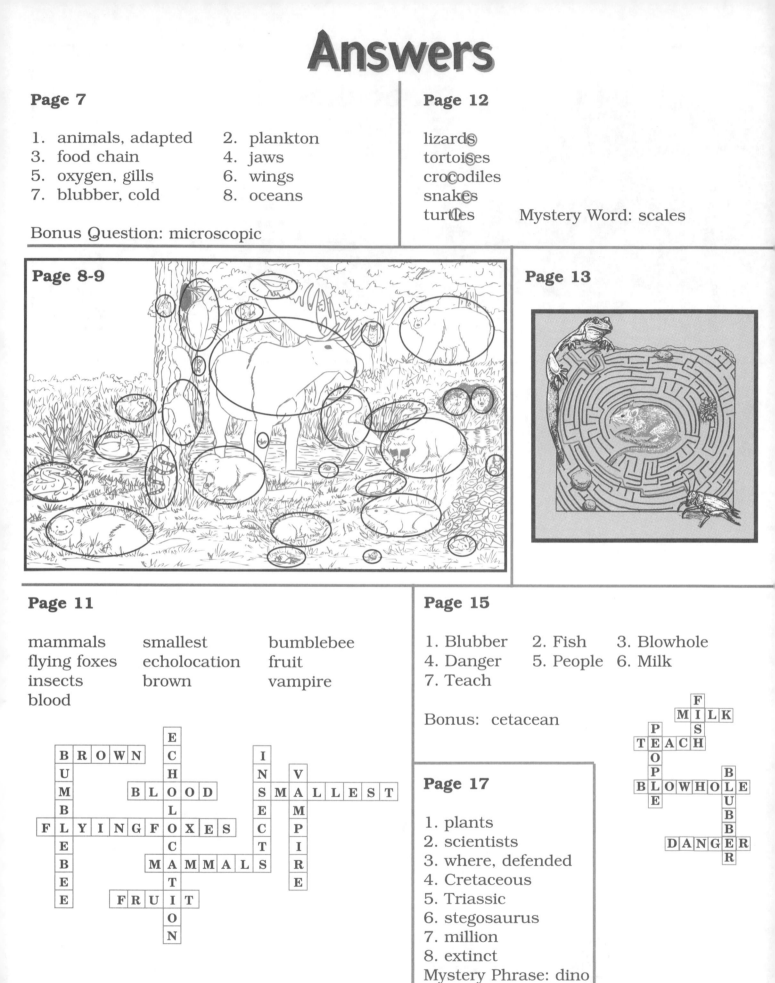

Page 11

mammals   smallest   bumblebee
flying foxes   echolocation   fruit
insects   brown   vampire
blood

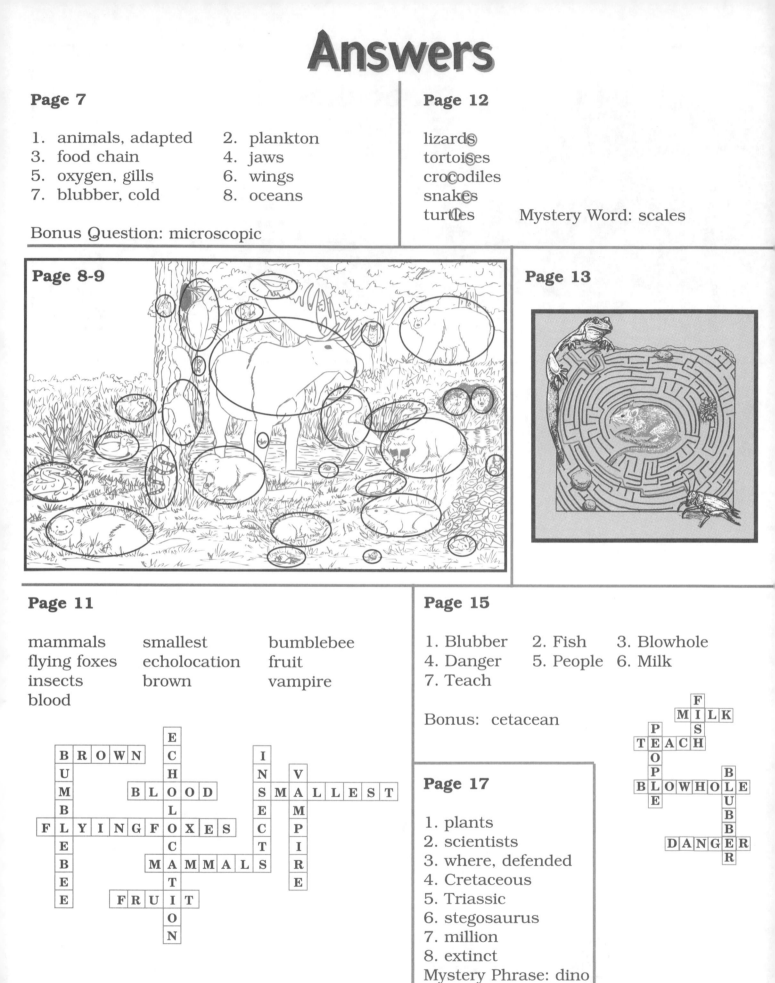

Page 15

1. Blubber   2. Fish   3. Blowhole
4. Danger   5. People   6. Milk
7. Teach

Bonus: cetacean

Page 17

1. plants
2. scientists
3. where, defended
4. Cretaceous
5. Triassic
6. stegosaurus
7. million
8. extinct
Mystery Phrase: dino power

Page 18

1. tarantula
2. garden spider
3. wandering
4. palps
5. eight eyes

Mystery Word: arachnids

Page 19

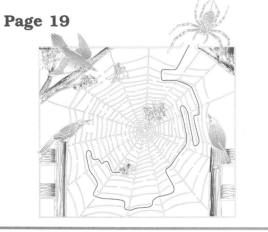

Page 20

1. alone
2. hibernation
3. roost
4. palm
5. tent-building bats
6. disk-winged bats
7. cave
8. drink
9. habitats
10 Texas

Bonus: Batman

Page 21

1. Magellanic
2. royal
3. yellow-eyed
4. emperor
5. chinstrap

Page 24

1. teeth
2. beaks
3. flat
4. crests
5. Cretaceous

Page 25

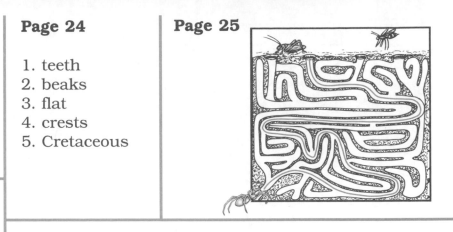

Page 26-27

Page 28

Page 22-23

Page 29

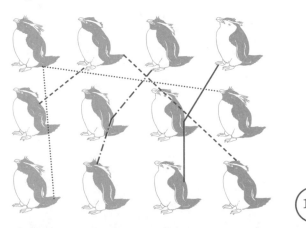

171

Page 30-31

Page 32

1. gray whales
2. bottlenose dolphins
3. blue whales
4. spotted dolphins

Page 33

Page 34

1. sting
2. living
3. seek
4. velvet
5. ticks, mites
6. eggs
7. arachnids
8. scorpion
9. helpful

Page 35

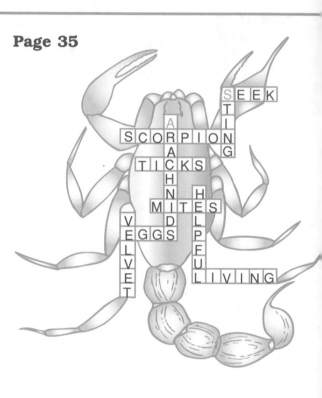

Page 36

Page 37

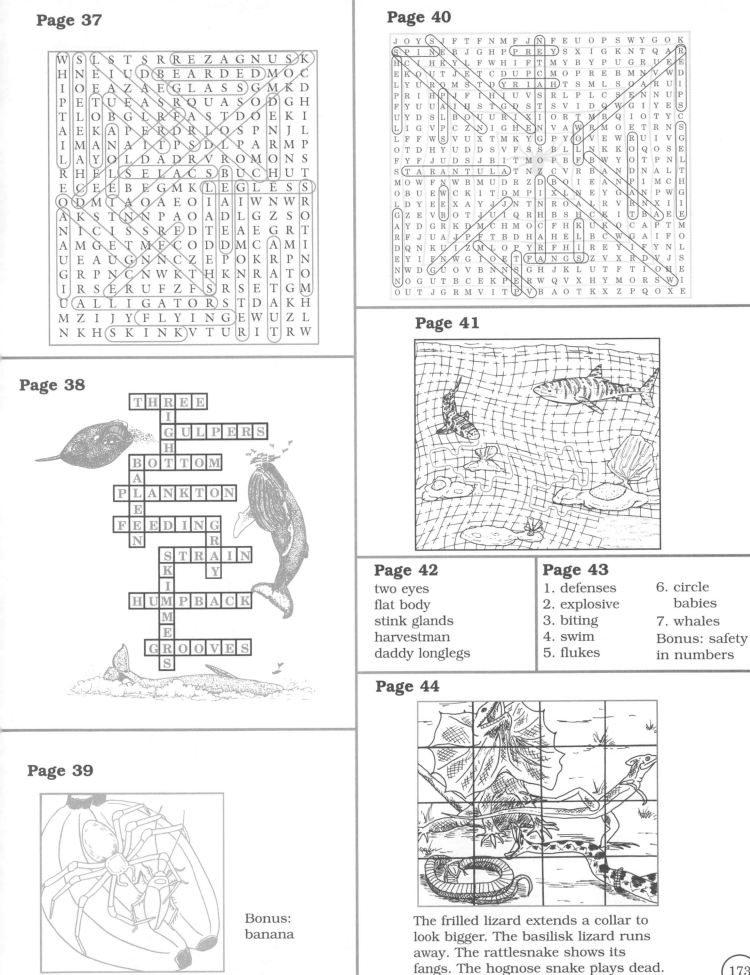

Page 38

Page 39

Bonus: banana

Page 40

Page 41

Page 42

two eyes
flat body
stink glands
harvestman
daddy longlegs

Page 43

1. defenses
2. explosive
3. biting
4. swim
5. flukes
6. circle babies
7. whales

Bonus: safety in numbers

Page 44

The frilled lizard extends a collar to look bigger. The basilisk lizard runs away. The rattlesnake shows its fangs. The hognose snake plays dead.

Page 45

1. coral; venomous; imitation
2. shed; tail; grow; tail
3. hides; shell; scaly; head
4. colored; poisonous

Page 46-47

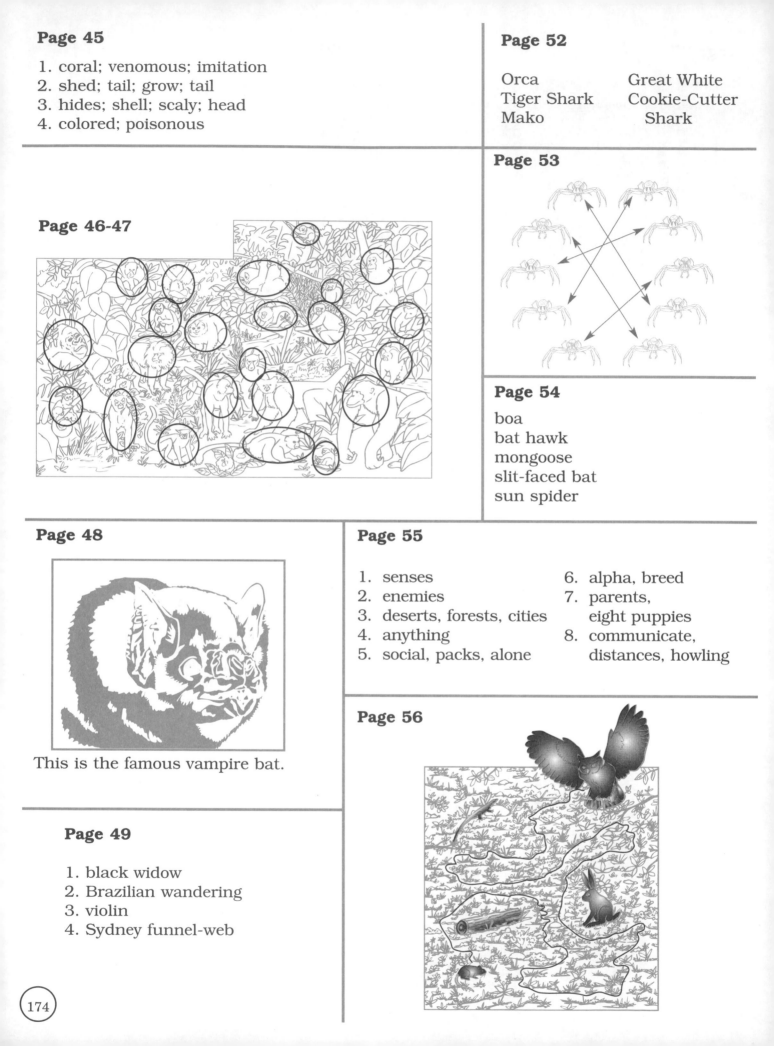

Page 48

This is the famous vampire bat.

Page 49

1. black widow
2. Brazilian wandering
3. violin
4. Sydney funnel-web

Page 52

Orca   Great White
Tiger Shark   Cookie-Cutter
Mako   Shark

Page 53

Page 54

boa
bat hawk
mongoose
slit-faced bat
sun spider

Page 55

1. senses
2. enemies
3. deserts, forests, cities
4. anything
5. social, packs, alone
6. alpha, breed
7. parents,
   eight puppies
8. communicate,
   distances, howling

Page 56

Page 57

1. Sharptail
2. Chain
3. Spotted
4. Green
5. Manytoothed

Page 59

predator
numbers
darkness
perches
moon
owl

growl
aggression
territory
flutter
box

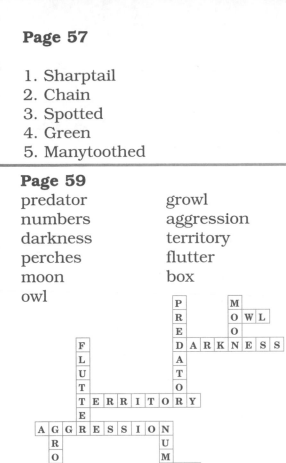

Page 61

1. willow leaf beetle
2. dogface
3. green darner
4. honey bee
5. bird grasshopper

Page 62

(word search grid)

Page 63

Page 64

1. giant panda
2. spectacled
3. black
4. grizzly
5. sun

Page 66

Across	Down
2. habitat	1. chase
3. hares	2. hunters
4. prey	4. plains
5. stalk	6. kitty
8. tiger	7. caracal
11. lynx	9. ocelot
12. lions	10. forest

Page 67

The whale is a gray whale, and it is breaching.

Page 68-69

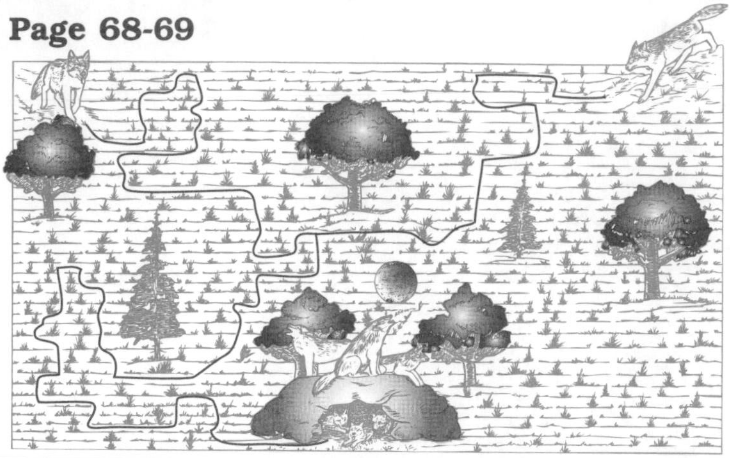

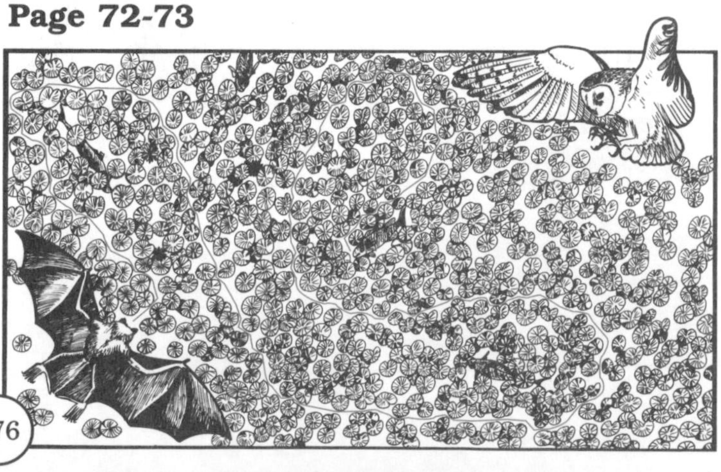

Page 74

Box   Gopher   Giant

Page 70

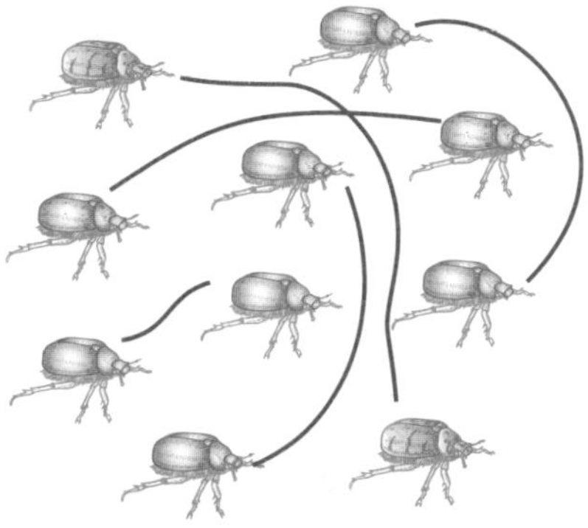

Page 75

Page 71

```
      L         S
      O         W
    P O R P O I S E S
      K         M
          M
        B A B I E S
          E
P     D       R
I   V A Q U I T A
G     L
F I N L E S S
I     S
S
H
```

Page 79

2. purse, web, burrow
3. green, lynx, venom
4. fishing, under, water
5. wolf, huntsman

```
            W
V E N O M   O
            L
      F I S H I N G
            U     R
            N     E
        L Y N X   E
            S     N
        P U R S E
            M   W
      C H A S E     P
            N   B U R R O W
                U   E
                N   Y
                D
                E
      W A T E R
```

Page 72-73

Page 80

Indo-Pacific   Nile

Siamese   American

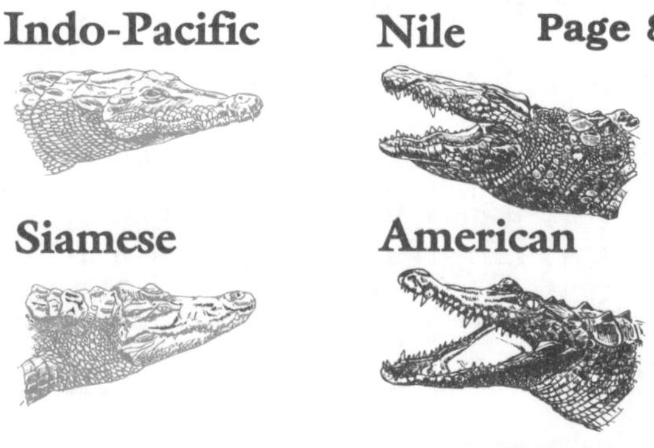

Page 81

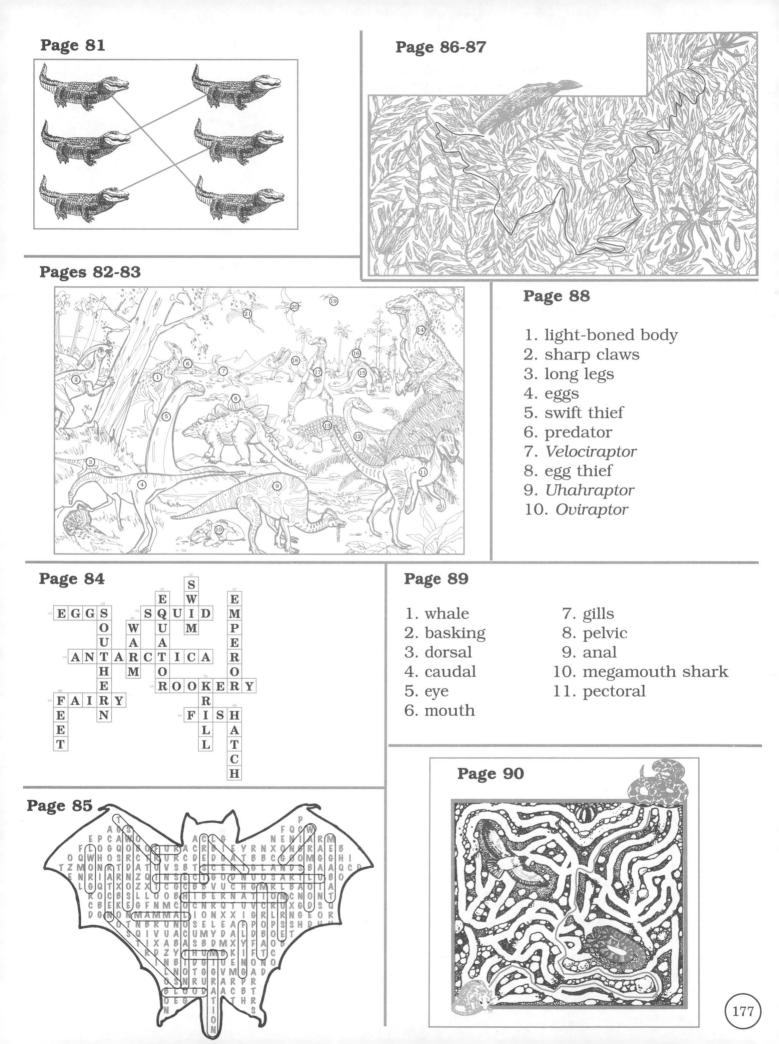

Pages 82-83

Page 86-87

Page 88

1. light-boned body
2. sharp claws
3. long legs
4. eggs
5. swift thief
6. predator
7. *Velociraptor*
8. egg thief
9. *Uhahraptor*
10. *Oviraptor*

Page 84

Page 89

1. whale	7. gills
2. basking	8. pelvic
3. dorsal	9. anal
4. caudal	10. megamouth shark
5. eye	11. pectoral
6. mouth	

Page 85

Page 90

Page 91

Northern India is home to the k<u>i</u>ng c<u>o</u>br<u>a</u>. An average ad<u>u</u>lt king cobra can gr<u>ow</u> to 15 f<u>ee</u>t long! V<u>e</u>ry aggressive, the king cobra may attack a p<u>erso</u>n without even being pr<u>o</u>voked. The king cobra is the only sn<u>a</u>ke to b<u>ui</u>ld a n<u>e</u>st for its <u>e</u>ggs. The m<u>o</u>th<u>er</u> gathers decaying leaves with the coils of her b<u>o</u>dy and g<u>ua</u>rds the <u>e</u>ggs for as long as 80 days until they h<u>a</u>tch.

Page 92-93

Page 94

ache	ail	ale	arch	arches
ark	back	bake	bail	balk
bark	beach	beak	bean	bin
black	blank	brick	brink	cab
canal	chain	chew	chin	chink
each	fail	fawn	finch	finches
fine	fish	fishes	flack	flake
flick	flinch	flinches	frisk	hack
hail	half	hawk	hewn	inch
inches	ink	kale	kiln	kin
knack	lack	lake	lane	lash
leach	leaf	leak	lean	leash
lick	link	nab	nail	nib
sack	sail	sale	sank	saw
scab	scale	seal	sew	shack
shale	shank	sheik	shelf	shin
sick	silk	sink	skin	slab
slack	slick	snack	snail	snake
sneak	swine	wail	walk	wane
wash	whale	whine	win	wine
wink	wish			...and more!

Page 95

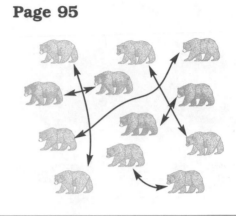

Page 96

Chinstrap Penguin

Page 97

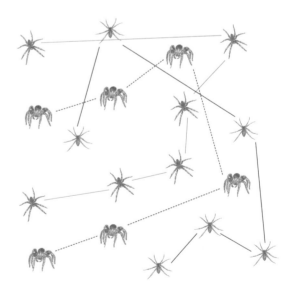

Page 98-99

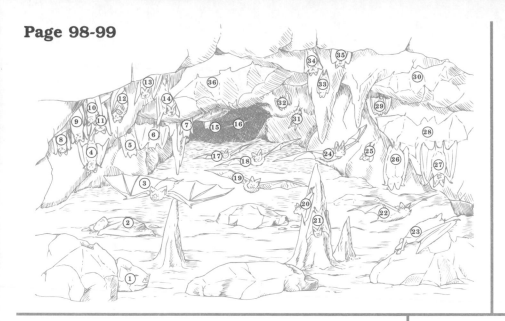

Page 102

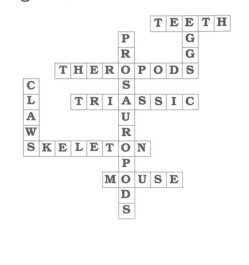

Page 100

Page 103

leafnose
bulldog
leaf-chinned
free-tailed
big-eared

Page 101

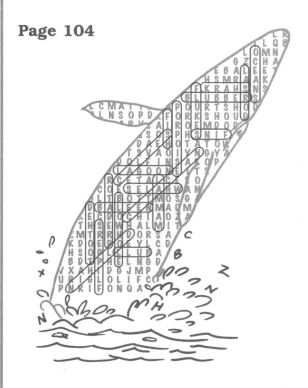

Page 104

Page 105

Across
2. twig
4. colony
7. antennae
9. scavengers
10. silk
11. ant

Down
1. mimic
3. motionless
5. beetle
6. net
8. predators
9. spiders

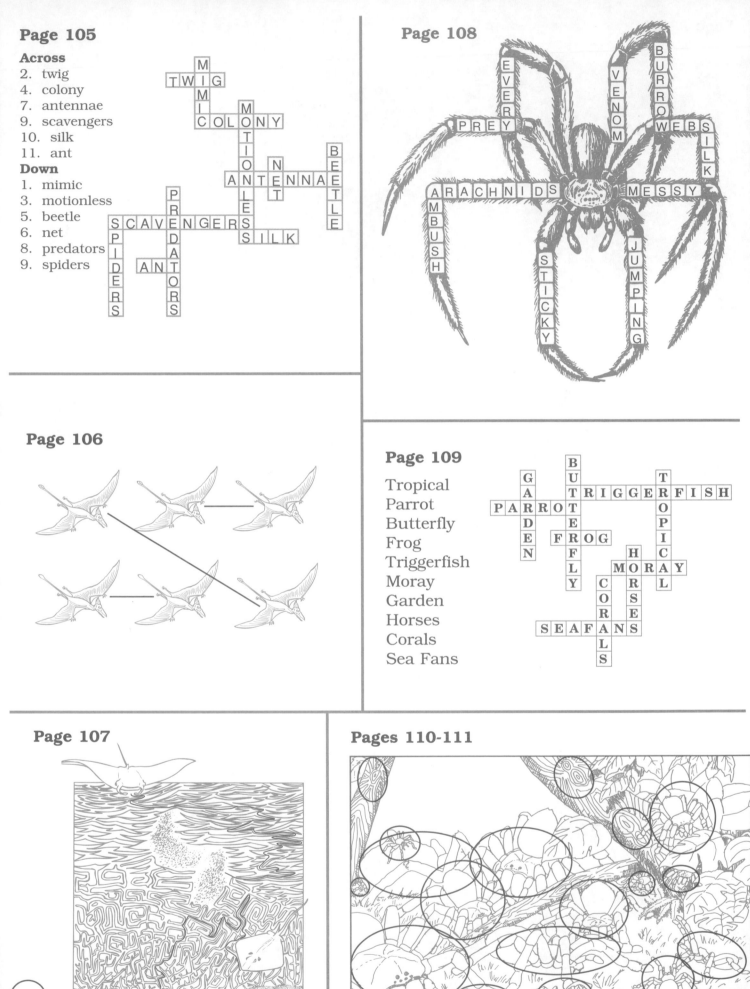

Page 108

Page 106

Page 109

Tropical
Parrot
Butterfly
Frog
Triggerfish
Moray
Garden
Horses
Corals
Sea Fans

Page 107

Pages 110-111

180

Page 112

1. Goosebeaked whale
2. Strap-tooth whale
3. Giant bottlenose whale
4. Archbeak whale

Page 113

pups
hairless
one month
nurseries
hunt

Page 114

Spectacled

Page 115

Page 116

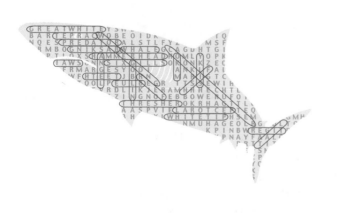

Page 117

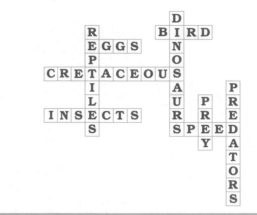

Pages 118-119

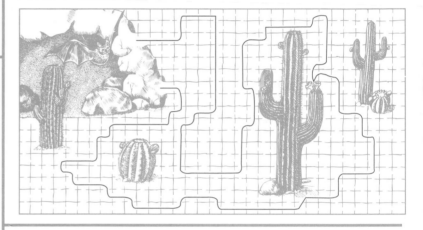

Page 120

1. run away, venom
2. drop, threatened
3. rearing up, fangs
Bonus: weavers

Page 121

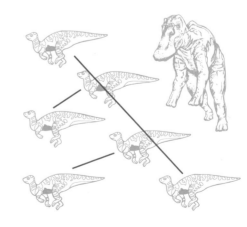

Page 122-123

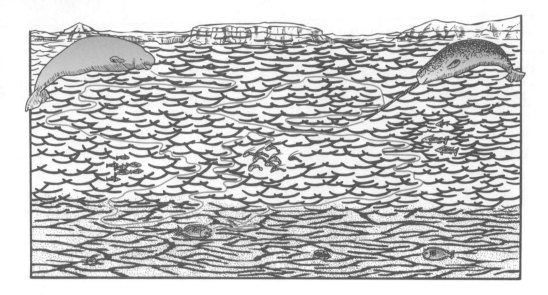

Page 125

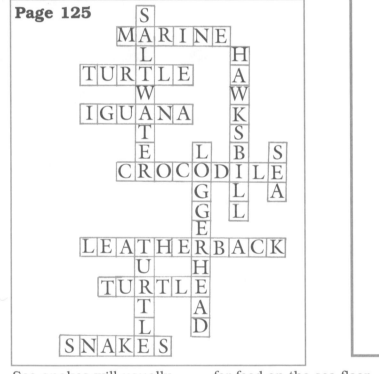

```
        S
   M A R I N E       H
T U R T L E          A
   L          W      W
I G U A N A          K
   W          L      S
   A      L          B   S
   C R O C O D I L E   E
   E      G   L      L   A
          G   L
   L E A T H E R B A C K
          U      E
   T U R T L E   H
          T      E
          L      A
   S N A K E S   D
```

Sea snakes will usually not bite unless you provoke them.
The saltwater crocodile is the only reptile of its kind that lives in the sea.
A real creature of the sea, the marine iguana, searches for food on the sea floor.
The hawksbill turtle has a beaklike upper jaw.
The leatherback turtle grows to be very big. Fishing nets are a real problem for the endangered loggerhead turtle.

Pages 126-127

1. Tiger Shark
2. Megamouth
3. Sawfish
4. Nurse Shark
5. Cookiecutter Shark
6. Skate
7. Thresher Shark
8. Ratfish
9. Dogfish Shark
10. Reef Shark
11. Wobbegong
12. Lemon Shark
13. Carpet Shark
14. Dwarf Shark
15. Nurse Shark
16. Blue Shark
17. Great White Shark
18. Bonnethead
19. Blue Shark
20. Eagle Ray
21. Whale Shark
22. Basking Shark
23. Bull Shark
24. Blue Shark
25. Dogfish Shark
26. Reef Shark

Page 128

ant, any, aunt, aura, nanny, nary, nasty, nor, nosy, not, nun, nut, oar, our, ran, rant, rat, ray, roar, roast, rosy, run, rust, rusty, sauna, say, soar, son, sour, soy, star, stay, stun, sty, sun, tan, tar, tarry, ton, toss, tour, toy, tray, truss, try, ...and many more!

Page 129

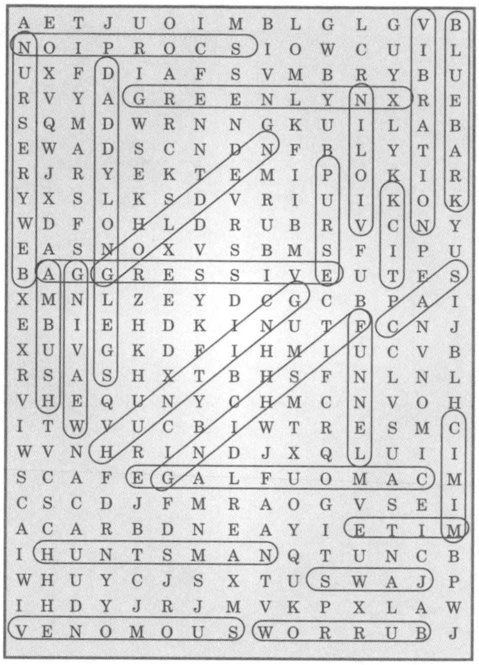

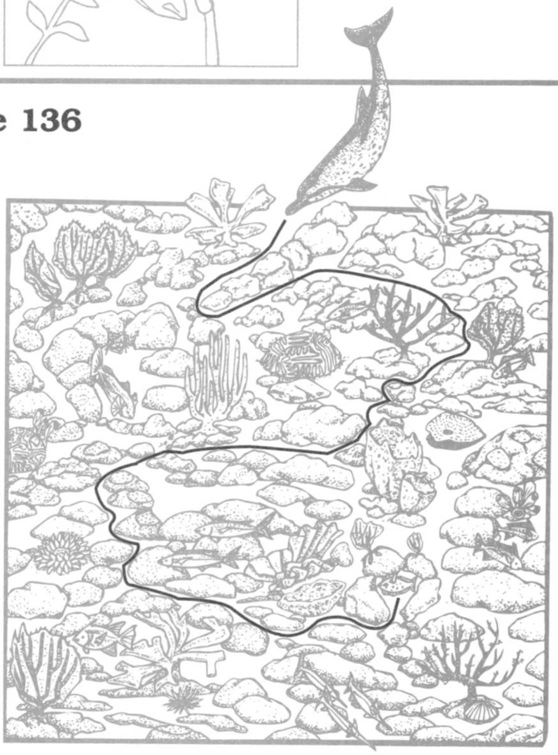

Pages 130-131
Here's one way to get there.

Page 132-133

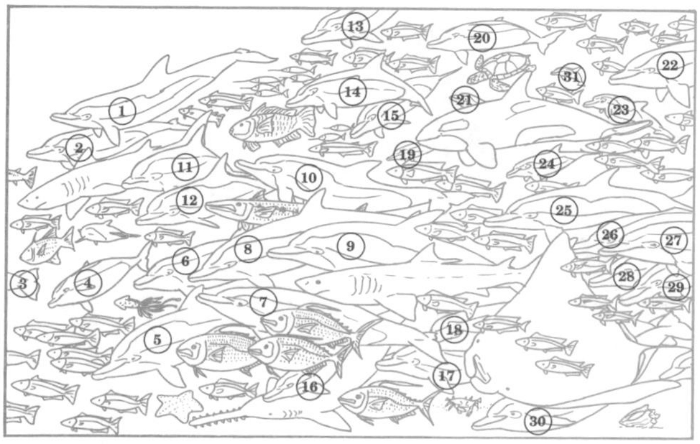

Page 134

1. claws
2. wings
3. finger bones
4. thumb claws
5. fur
6. nose leaves
7. large ears
8. thin skin
9. sharp teeth
10. eyes

Page 135

Page 136

Page 137

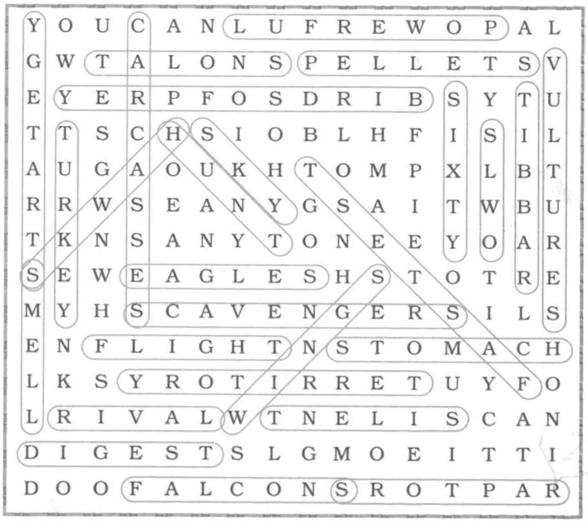

Pages 138-139

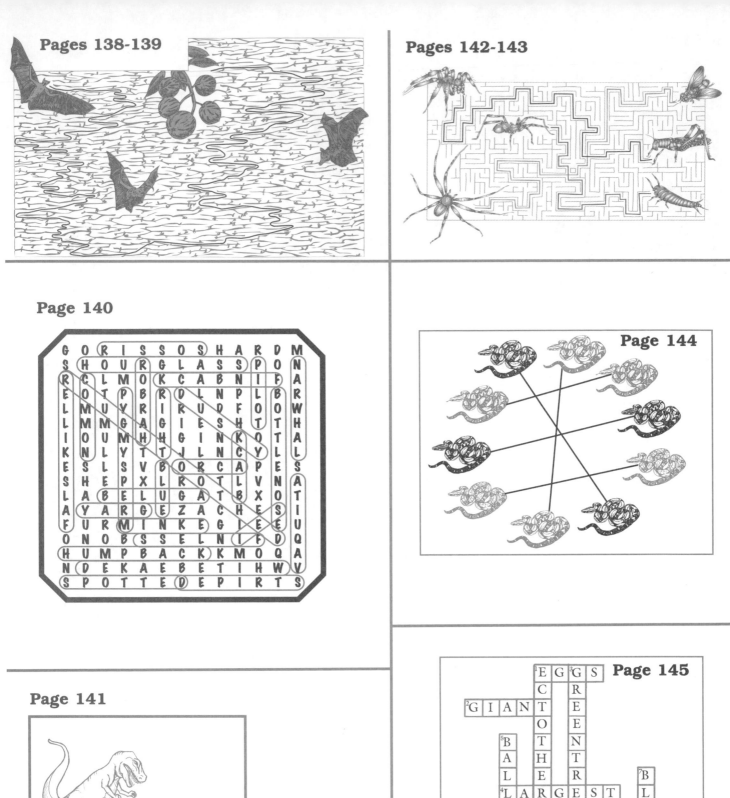

Pages 142-143

Page 140

```
G O R I S S O S H A R D O M
S H O U R G L A S S P I N A
R C O L M R O K C A B N L R
E O T U O B R R I D N F H W
L M P Y G M A H T V X K H C A
L O U G M Y S P I J L O R A L
I N M L E P X B L U C A T A S
K S U M R G E Z A C H L T A
E A Y A R M I N K E G N T I
S L F U R M I N K E G N T I
L F O N O B S S E L N E I F Q
A O H U M P B A C K K M O Q A
F N D E K A E B E T I H W V
S S P O T T E D E P I R T S
```

Page 144

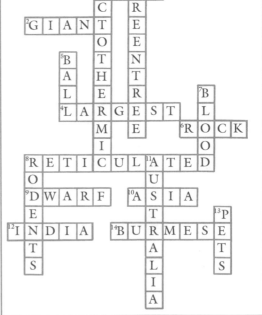

Page 141

TYRANNOSAURUS REX
AND
TRICERATOPS

Page 145

```
           ¹E G G ³S
           C     R
  ²G I A N T     E
           O     E
        ⁵B T     N
        A  H     T
        L  E     R    ⁷B
  ⁴L A R G E S T      L
        M  I     ⁶R O C K
        I           O
  ⁸R E T I C U L ¹¹A T E D
  O        U        D
  ⁹D W A R F  ¹⁰A S I A
  E        S
  ¹²I N D I A  ¹⁴B U R M E S E T  ¹³P
  N        T              E
  T        R              T
  S        A              S
           L
           I
           A
```

Pages 146-147

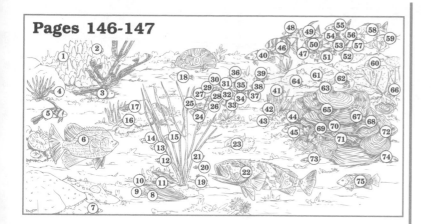

Page 152
Bottlenose dolphin

Page 148

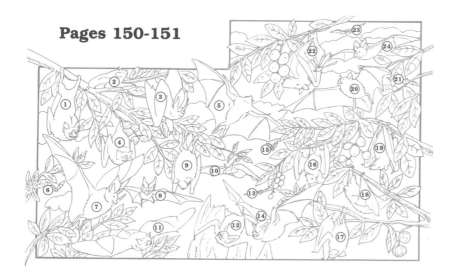

Page 153

Pages 150-151

Pages 154-155

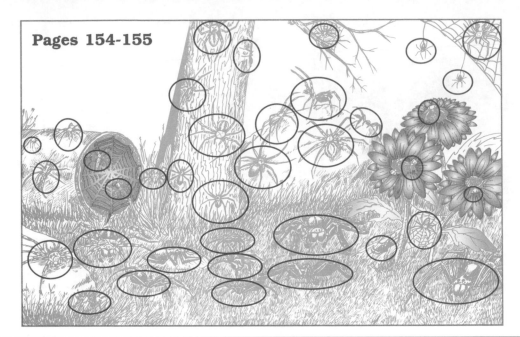

Page 156

Pages 157
Siberian Tiger

Page 159
Here are 50 possibilities:

add	drip	pig	spin
and	ear	pine	spine
anger	end	rain	spree
dad	green	read	spring
danger	grin	riders	sweep
dare	grind	ring	swing
dig	nag	ringer	wander
diner	nine	sand	wasp
dip	pad	send	win
drain	paid	side	wind
drape	pain	singer	wing
draw	pie	sip	
dress	pies	speed	

Pages 160-161

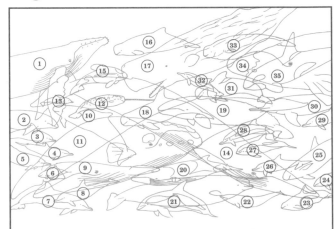

Page 162

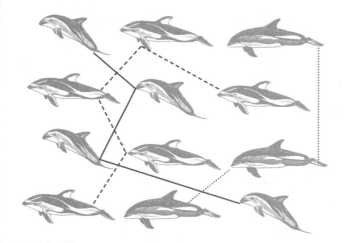

Page 163

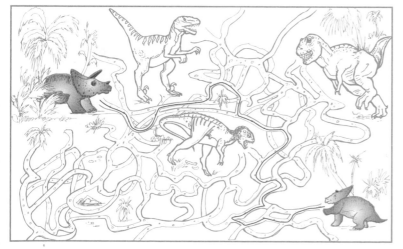

Pages 164-165

Page 166

Here are 50 possibilities:

aim	bet	mate	spire	step
ape	bit	mite	spit	stair
are	imp	pat	spite	stare
aspire	irate	pet	sprite	tab
ate	ire	pie	stab	tap
bar	item	pit	stamp	tape
bare	map	same	stave	vase
bat	mar	seam	starve	viral
beam	mast	smart	steam	vista
beat	mat	spat	stem	vital

Page 168

1. poison
2. slow; preys; run away
3. coloration; predators

BONUS: desert

Page 169

Glossary

algae *(AL-jee)* tiny water plants, including seaweed, that contain chlorophyll; *p. 124*

alpha *(AL-fuh)* the dominant animal in a group; *p. 55*

antennae *(an-TEH-nee)* sensory organs on the head of an insect or other animal; *p. 105*

arachnids *(uh-RAK-nidz)* a class of animals that includes spiders, scorpions, mites, and ticks; *p. 18*

baleen *(buh-LEEN)* rows of bristled plates that hang from the upper jaws of many types of whale; *p. 38*

blowhole *(BLOH-hole)* a nostril on the top of the head of a whale or other cetacean; *p. 7*

breaching *(BREE-ching)* leaping out of water; *p. 43*

breed *(BREED)* to mate; *p. 55*

camouflage *(KAH-muh-flaj)* to hide by covering something or changing the way it looks; *p. 36*

carapace *(KAR-uh-payce)* a spider's hard, protective covering; *p. 97*

carcass *(KAR-kus)* the dead body of an animal; *p. 137*

cetaceans *(sih-TAY-shun)* a group of aquatic marine mammals; *p. 14*

cow *(KOW)* a female whale; *p. 43*

crèche *(KRESH)* penguin nursery; *p. 156*

dominant *(DOM-uh-nunt)* controlling; *p. 55*

dorsal fin *(DOR-sul fin)* large fin on the upper back of a fish or cetacean; *p. 50*

echolocation *(eh-koh-loh-KAY-shun)* the process of finding things in the dark using sound waves; *p. 10*

environment *(in-VY-run-munt)* natural surroundings, including air, land, water, plants, and animals; *p. 10*

extinction *(ik-STING-shun)* no longer existing; *p. 13*

flukes *(FLOOKS)* the two "wings" on the tail of a whale or dolphin; *p. 43*

fossil *(FAH-sul)* the remains of a plant or an animal preserved in earth or rocks; *p. 17*

habitat *(HA-buh-tat)* the area where an animal naturally lives; *p. 13*

hibernate *(HY-bur-nayt)* to pass the winter in a sleeping state; *p. 20*

lagoon *(luh-GOON)* a shallow body of water connected to a larger, deeper body of water; *p. 32*

marine *(muh-REEN)* of or relating to the sea; *p. 7*

microscopic *(my-kruh-SKAH-pik)* very small; invisible without the use of a microscope; *p. 7*

migrate *(MY-grate)* travel to another place for feeding or breeding; *p. 20*

mollusks *(MAH-lusks)* group of animals with soft bodies usually covered by shells, including snails, clams, and squids; *p. 122*

orca *(OR-kuh)* killer whale; *p. 51*

paleontologist *(pay-lee-on-TAH-luh-jist)* a scientist who studies fossils; *p. 17*

palps *(PALPS)* leglike structures near a spider's mouth that hold prey while the spider feeds; *p. 18*

parasites *(PAIR-uh-syte)* plant or animal that lives in, with, or on another plant or animal; *p. 34*

pectoral fin *(PEK-tuh-rul fin)* fin located on the side, toward the front, of a marine animal such as a shark, dolphin, or whale; *p. 51*

pellet *(PEH-let)* a lump of material that an owl coughs up, containing fur, bones, teeth, and other things that the owl's body can't digest; *p. 137*

pelvic fin *(PEL-vik fin)* a fin located on the side, toward the back, of a marine animal such as a shark, dolphin, or whale; *p. 51*

plankton *(PLANK-tun)* tiny animals and plants living in the sea that are the basic food for larger sea animals; *p. 7*

pod *(POD)* herd of whales; *p. 32*

predator *(PREH-duh-tur)* an animal that hunts other animals for food; *p. 6*

prey *(PRAY)* an animal that is hunted by other animals for food; *p. 7*

scavenger *(SKAH-vun-jur)* an animal that feeds on the dead bodies of other animals; *p. 105*

Southern Hemisphere *(SUH-thurn HE-muh-sfeer)* the southern half of the Earth, located below the equator; *p. 84*

species *(SPEE-sheez)* a particular type or kind of animal; *p. 10*

spiderling *(SPY-der-ling)* baby spider; *p. 53*

strategy *(STRAH-tuh-jee)* a careful plan or method; *p. 137*

talon *(TAH-lun)* the sharp curving claw of a bird of prey; *p. 137*

temperate *(TEM-puh-rut)* having a moderate temperature; *p. 89*

territory *(TER-uh-tor-ee)* the area that an animal controls; *p. 59*

ultrasound *(UL-truh-saund)* sound waves used for *echolocation*. Ultrasound cannot be heard by human beings; *p. 85*

venom *(VEH-num)* poison spread by an animal through stinging or biting; *p. 18*

wingspan *(WING-span)* the distance from the tip of one wing to the tip of the other; *p. 11*